Unleash your mind, become a sales warrior, and earn what you're truly worth.

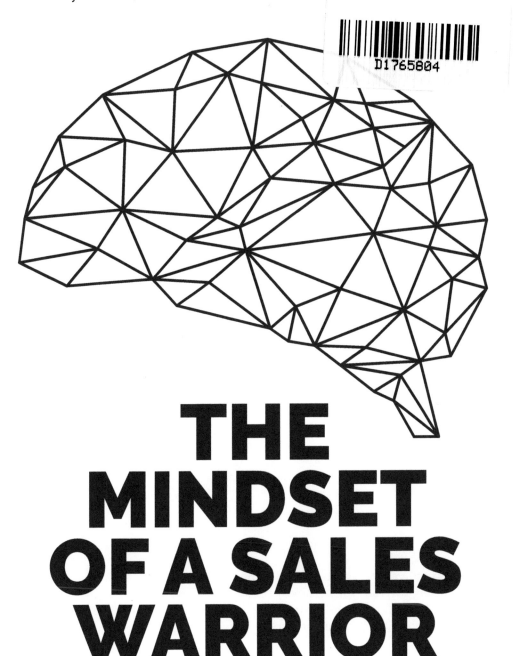

THE MINDSET OF A SALES WARRIOR

JASON FORREST

Printed in U.S.A

International Standard Book Number: 978-1-64669-142-5

TABLE OF CONTENTS

A WARRIOR SEND OFF

The journey you're about to embark on in this book will strengthen your ability to accomplish three primary objectives so you can earn what you're truly worth.

First, you'll increase your goal clarity. These mental strategies will give you the ability to declutter your mind, identify your goals, and give yourself total certainty around them. You can't achieve anything until you know what you want.

Second, you'll increase your motivation around your goals. Nobody achieves anything great unless they have an internally-fueled drive to do, achieve, and conquer. You'll know how to have an internal engine of endless energy that you can refuel any time you want.

Finally, you'll do the work to remove the hidden leashes that hold you back from earning what you're truly worth. By solidifying your goal clarity, increasing your motivation, and removing your leashes, you'll become the sales warrior you were created to be.

ACKNOWLEDGMENTS

A special thank you to **Mary Marshall Forrest**, for being my wife, president of FPG, and my 24/7 partner in every area of my life. Thank you for spending countless hours refining my message as my production editor and making this book what it is. Lastly, thank you for our unscripted conversations and bringing the concepts to life in the audiobook. My life is better with you.

Will Parchman, for being the senior editor, and helping me craft and research my message. Your role on this project was invaluable.

Jacqui Faber, for being my publicist, and for providing the research to back up our philosophies.

Remington May, for overseeing the project design.

Spiros Vithoulkas, for creating the layout and cover of the book.

Susan Stageman, my NLP Yoda, for helping me master many of the applications in this book.

To the FPG trainers, for providing feedback for the book: **Maria Gonzalez Bartov**, **Rachel Castor**, **Tracye McCarthy**, and **Melissa Turba**.

All of the **employees of FPG** who provide such an incredible example for the world of what it means to be a sales warrior.

To my mentors who gave me guidance during our writer's week retreat: **Kris Frieswick**, **Michael O'Brien**, **Susan Stageman,** and **Richard Tiller**.

And lastly, to everyone who engaged with us on social media and helped us mold this book into its final form. Thank you.

DEDICATION

This book is dedicated to all the men and women in the sales profession who are on the battlefield every day fighting the sales war on all fronts. This book is for you.

THE GROUNDWORK FOR AN UNLEASHED LIFE

As my senior year of college drew to a close, I was preparing to finish my academic career and jump into the real world. At the time, I was taking a class from a marketing professor who I deeply respected, and one day the topic of conversation in his class turned to job opportunities. We were all on the verge of beginning our professional lives, and we were peppering him with questions about various job fields.

I remember someone specifically asking this experienced, respected professor, "What about a career in sales?" His response hit me like a gut punch.

"Sales is no place for a college graduate."

I had grown up around the sales profession. My father was the owner of the oldest and most successful jewelry store in North Dallas. I'd seen him improve the lives of thousands of people. But now I was hit by an internal storm of conflict that challenged everything I thought I knew about sales. It leashed me to some degree in the sense that it gave me a level of role rejection. Now I wasn't sure sales was so great after all. And I knew that if I could be made to feel this way after deeply admiring the profession for so long, how easy would it be to create an entire tribe of people who thought sales was beneath them?

In other words, modern sales warriors are under siege.

This book is for any sales warrior who wants to get more out of their life than they're currently getting.You may be a frontline salesperson in outside or inside sales looking to create more abundance in your life. You may be an entrepreneur looking to amplify your ideas to the world. You may be a salesmanager in search of coaching resources to unleash your team's performance. You may be an executive looking for strategies to push your company to the next level. Or maybe you're considering a career in sales, and you want to startthe next phase of your life with the mentality you need to join the top 1%.

"80% OF ALL SALESPEOPLE ARE EITHER FIRED OR QUIT WITHIN THE FIRST YEAR AT A JOB."

Wherever you are in your career right now, I've written this book for you. It applies to the mind andthe soul of the best part of all of us. It speaks directly to your ability to have a mindset that actively works for you, both consciously and subconsciously.

To understand why this is so vitally important, I want you to step inside the shoes of the average salesperson and experience what they see, hear, and feel.

Friends tell you that you work too hard because they never see you. Your family asks whether you took a sales job as a stepping stone to management, because no one would actually want a career in sales. Your manager tells you he's going to hire someone else if you don't meet your quota. Other departments tell you that you're an overpaid prima donna. Your peers tell you that the only reason you make sales is that you're lucky. Your prospects tell you that you're charging too much for what you're selling. And your customers tell you that you need to get your customer service department in check or they're going with the competition.

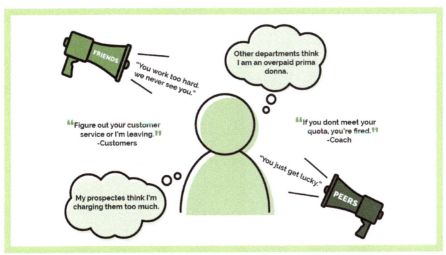

It's a constant onslaught, to the point that 80% of all salespeople are either fired or quit within the first year at a job. Salespeople are constantly fighting a war on all fronts, taking fire from customers and prospects from the front and friendly fire from family and friends from the back. Up until today, this has been an impossible mental war to win.

Not anymore. Welcome to your new sales warrior mindset.

A sales warrior mindset is the foundation of your success. The goal is to integrate psychological, physical, and tactical training to add dimensions to your life that often get overlooked. These dimensions are vital to achieve maximum performance in any skill, not just sales. A sales warrior mindset isn't a hat you put on when you start your day and take off when working hours are over. A sales warrior mindset is embedded into your programming, a strength that's woven into every aspect of your life.

This book isn't about making things easier for you. It's about making you better by strengthening your mindset to such a degree that none of those outer stories matter. And that means embodying the mind of a true sales warrior.

This also isn't a book about changing the circumstances around you. That's external culture. Our programs at FPG focus on transforming that culture to create more productivity that encourages achievement. Instead, this book is about building up an internal, individual belief system for selling that is so strong that nothing gets through your armor.

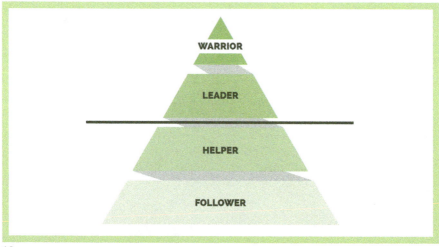

To explain exactly what I mean by a sales warrior, I created a pyramid called The Levels of a Sales Warrior.

The follower level is the most passive of the levels. They're afraid to initiate contact, afraid to lead the sale, afraid to ask for the close. This all stems from the fear that something you do or say or not know will actually hurt your chances of a sale. There's no shame in being on the follower level. We all start there. But the key is that you can't stay here and be successful. You need to actively look for ways to move up.

The helper level has become increasingly common over the last century – these are salespeople who view themselves as "relationship managers" or "consultants," ready to respond if the prospect needs anything but don't do any real assertive selling of the value of what they offer. Helpers are there to help the prospect if they need anything but operate on a purely reactive basis. Their positive intention is pure – they just want to help. The problem with this is that our research shows that only about 5% of prospects ask for help. The other 95% need it but never actively ask for it, so that's a lot of money left on the table and lives left unchanged if all you're doing is letting prospects come to you.

Then you have the leader. The leader is focused on guiding the prospect all along the way. They lead, and as a result, they have no problem hitting their sales quotas. This is not a bad place to be, but at the end of the day, leaders look up to the President's Club members and wonder, "How do I get there?" Leaders view their sales job as a career and a profession, which is awesome. But there's still one level higher.

At the top of the pyramid, you have the sales warrior, who believes sales isn't just a career; it's a mission. Southwest Airlines calls this a "warrior spirit," someone who works hard, desires to be the best, and is courageous.

The sales warrior is defined by one key attribute – they believe their entire philosophy about selling is that all human beings move away from pain and toward life improvement, and a sales warrior's mission is to liberate them from any indecision.

Like the leader, a sales warrior knows their product or service, and actively initiates conversations to educate prospects on how that product or service will improve their life. But the sales warrior goes on to also know their competition, and what happens if the prospect chooses to do nothing. The sales warrior feels freedom in guiding others, knows they are helping improve the lives of those they serve, and earns what they are truly worth for doing it.

I believe that the number one desire of the human race is freedom, and the sales warrior is on a quest to give freedom and liberate their prospect from making the wrong decision. And here's the important part – that leadership always comes from a place of love, not fear.

A sales warrior is the primary source of confidence, motivation, hope, and certainty in the prospect's decision to buy or not buy. A sales warrior believes every prospect they meet wants to be sold to, because they don't just want life improvement; they need it. A sales warrior believes that sales is the most noble profession in the world, a vehicle to dramatically improve the lives of every one of their prospects.

A sales warrior is the protector of their prospect's mission to improve their lives. They're protecting them from making the wrong decision and guiding them toward total freedom. That's the most noble goal I can imagine.

I get asked all the time how salespeople become a follower, or a helper, or a leader, or a sales warrior. Everything comes from The Results Matrix.

Sales is the worst paying 9-5 job on the planet. Want to know why? Because it's not 9-5. Salespeople are asked to work nights, weekends and major holidays, and sales warriors use that time to make worth-it money, not 9-5 money. Worth-it money means you can justify missing all those happy hours with friends. It means missing weekend birthday parties or family gatherings and feeling like it's worth it. In order to do that, you need the right programming, beliefs, emotions, motivation, and behaviors. You can't make worth-it money until you have warrior programming and warrior beliefs, and that's where the Results Matrix comes in.

Here's how it works.

The reason you make the money you do is because of your everyday behaviors. It's because of what you do on a daily basis. Salespeople who make 9-5 money are reactive. They wait for prospects to come to them. They wait for their prospects to ask questions. They wait for their manager to initiate their training so they can add more resources and make more money. A sales warrior who makes worth-it money is proactive in finding prospects. They are relentless in uncovering objections. They have no fear of talking about the competition. They are hungry for training and demand coaching.

The reason you behave the way you do is because of the motivation behind your behaviors. Someone who's earning 9-5 money has a have-to motivation. Their self-talk sounds like, "I have to go to work today. I have to follow this sales process. I have to sell this product or service. I have to have this sales job." A sales warrior making worth-it money has a want-to motivation. They want to be challenged to find new ways to improve peoples' lives. They want to make sure everyone on earth can buy from them today over all alternatives. They want to convince others to have a better life today than they had yesterday.

Your motivation comes from your emotions. I believe that all emotions stem from love or fear. If someone's making 9-5 money, it's because of fear. They fear there aren't enough buyers out there. They fear that the prospect might not be happy with their product or service. They fear questions they don't know the answers to. Sales warriors who make worth-it money are proactive because their emotions are rooted in love. That leads to total advocacy for their prospect. Love means they want their prospects to have resolution and not ambiguity. Love means they are a protector of their company's mission and vision. Love means they revere the sales profession as a vehicle for life improvement.

Your emotions come from your beliefs. Someone who's earning 9-5 money has an "I am not enough" belief system. They scream in the form of alibis and excuses. When something goes wrong, they operate from a place of shame and not guilt. They believe they are the mistake as opposed to believing they made a mistake. A sales warrior who's earning worth-it money has an "I am enough" belief system. They listen. They're receptive to coaching, and they believe everything they need to be successful is within them now. They have an unshakeable belief that they are the problem, but they are also the solution.

Your beliefs come from your programming, which form the root of who you are at your core. Someone making 9-5 money is programmed with a fixed mindset. They believe they are as good as they'll ever be right now. They believe they were born with a certain set of skills, and they can't add new ones. They believe that the amount of money they make now is the best they can ever do. A sales warrior making worth-it money has a growth mindset. They believe they can grow and add new strategies and learn new things every day. They are freed from the tyranny of perfectionism. They believe in excellence, in being better than they were yesterday. They believe that positive change always comes from adding more resources.

All of the activities in this book are positively programming you. The purpose is to take control of your programming so you can change your identity to become a sales warrior. The goal is not to say, "I have a sales job," but to say, "I AM a sales warrior." Instead of seeing sales as just a 9-5 job, what would happen if you committed to using this book to make worth-it money? What would happen if you added these resources to your consciousness and committed to earning what you're truly worth?

On a mindset level, everyone is constantly in one of four states about where they are in their life. This isn't who you are, and it doesn't define you, but you need to have awareness about your current mentality before you can do anything about it

My current life situation is:

1. A product of chance.
2. A product of programming and upbringing.
3. A product of my beliefs.
4. A product of my beliefs *and* my programming.

People who believe their current life situation is a product of chance are like a log tossed into a rushing river. Wherever the river takes them is where they've ended up. Whatever happens to them was completely out of their control; they're merely a witness to their own life experience. People like this believe everything in their life is happening to them, not for them.

A prospect says no? "Well, they weren't going to buy anyway, there is nothing I can do about it." An objection pops up? "I knew they weren't interested." It's all mindset.

Your programming refers to your patterns of thinking that have been built from the past events in your life. From the day you were born, your brain has been programmed by your environment, relationships, and experiences, and it has molded the way you think. Some of this programming is great. Maybe you had parents who taught you to respect and value the opinions of others. That's positive programming. But it's equally possible you've had people in your life give you negative programming that harms you.

Maybe you were taught, "buyers are liars," and that influences the way you act around and sell to your buyers. As we later dive into programming, I'll ask you to evaluate where certain aspects are leashing you from selling more or unleashing you to sell more.

People who blindly live their lives by their negative programming become slaves to that programming. They live life automatically, reacting to situations as the maps in their brain tell them to. Essentially, they believe they are helpless when it comes to the ability to change their fate. The thoughts that take over are, "This is just the way I was raised," or, "This is the hand I was dealt, I'm just not as lucky as others."

That programming ends up feeding into their beliefs about themselves. If you've been programmed by a manager who told you that customers don't trust salespeople, then your beliefs will reflect that; you'll gradually adopt that belief as one of your own without any deeper examination. That ends up influencing your actions, and the cycle spins.

It's only the people who combine their unleashed beliefs and their positive programming who truly become life's sales warriors. Belief without programming is wishful thinking. Programming without belief is circumstantial thinking. Belief combined with programming is warrior thinking.
Beliefs that build you up are important. You need to visualize success, affirm your own ability to achieve success, and fundamentally believe you're capable of being your own support, inspiration, and love. But you also need to address your programming as well. These are things like the automatic triggers you experience when you hear an objection from your prospect. Or the goals you subconsciously lock onto that don't fulfill your positive intention to keep growing and improving. That's programming, and you need that to be in alignment as well.

Someone whose programming is supported by negative beliefs will behave in ways that correspond with those beliefs. If they wake up every morning believing that they'll never be enough, because the people around them have told them so, they'll never live up to their full potential.

Maybe you had a rough childhood. Maybe you got let go from your job at a tough time in your life. Maybe you experienced a brutal heartbreak, and you were programmed negatively in some way by that moment. But guess what? Everyone's dealing with something. It's completely human to feel pushed down by circumstance, but you need to get back up. The difference between everyone else and a warrior, is that a warrior gets back up and finds the strength to overpower any negative past programming and become more.

Throughout your journey with this book, you'll learn about the mindset underneath the helmet of the sales warrior to align your beliefs with your programming. Your programming is everything you've learned, understood or experienced in your past that created the person you are today. It's like the mental lens that you use to see the world around you. But a sales warrior doesn't just realize they have that lens, they make a conscious decision to change the lens to see the world as a vehicle they can use to improve their lives and the lives of their prospects. The lens is no longer a crutch, it's a goal-seeking weapon.

Within these pages, you'll learn how to embody those beliefs and change that programming to overcome any challenge in front of you for the rest of your life.

In the process, you'll become the ultimate mind hacker. You'll have the power to bend any circumstance to meet your will. And you'll find that when you do this, and truly commit to the strategies you'll find in this book, you'll become a better version of yourself and a true sales warrior.

TAKE THE LEAP

Life is nothing more than a series of decisions, and this book represents one of those decisions. These words were written for you, because I know that you deserve to live your best life possible. I've known what it's like to want more, but not know how to get it. I've known what it's like to feel like you've hit a dead end. I've known what it's like to face rejections and setbacks.

We're all there at one point or another. But just like me, you have the power to change your circumstances. And you start by changing your mindset.

One thing I know from experience is that small improvements add up to big change. Embodying just one or two of the belief statements in this book will change you in some way that will benefit your life. But embodying all of them will transform you forever.

Again, life is nothing more than a series of decisions. You have a huge one staring at you right now as you prepare to go through this book. So, make these steps your strategy for encountering this book in the most powerful way possible.

1. Make a decision that you want more out of your life than you're currently getting.

2. As you go through these strategies, commit to following through, doing the work, and applying the concepts.

3. Continually come back to this book and use it as your mental energy source. Pull from individual chapters to build up your mental power, so you can conquer any challenge you face in life.

4. If you decide you want even more strategies to become unleashed, visit our book page at **www.themindsetofasaleswarrior.com** for more information about our game-changing mindset masterclass and resources.

My hope for you with this book is that you use it to transform your mindset about your sales, which will transform your reality, your results, and your life in the process. I challenge you to commit, be all in, and take the leap.

Here's to becoming a better version of you.

Jason

THE PRESUPPOSITIONS OF SALES WARRIOR'S MINDSET

1. There's no such thing as a business problem. There are personal problems that affect our business.

Yes, this book is about sales. It's about earning what you're truly worth by living with an unbreakable mindset at work and with customers. But to do that, you have to dive down to the root cause of what's really happening in your mind.

As much as we like to believe our personal lives are separate from our jobs, our personal problems leak into our professional lives and keep us from achieving what we're capable of. For example, if you have a hard time with conflict in your personal life, of course that will affect your sales career. The key is understanding that mindset so you can change it.

2. Positive change always comes from adding more resources.

Whatever you're getting right now, is equal to what you're currently doing. And what you're currently doing, is equal to your current mindset. If you want to change what you're getting, you must change what you're doing. And if you want to change what you're currently doing, you must change your mindset.

Everything in this book is an added mental resource, and these resources will only benefit you and add more to your life. As with anything, all you have to do to get better is learn more and apply what you've learned. The more you commit to living by these resources, the more your life will positively change. Embracing that truth is your pathway to becoming the sales warrior.

3. Frustration plus confusion is on the edge of a breakthrough.

Here's a caution. In life, we're so used to frustration and confusion being rejected because it throws us in a state of discomfort. Think about the first time you tried something completely new and terrifying, but ended up loving it. I'm sure you were nervous, I'm sure you had doubts, but once you took that leap you couldn't go back to your life before that jump.

"EMBRACE THE SUCK."

Embrace the frustration and confusion, because it means you're on the verge of something incredible. It's going to be hard, but as they commonly say in the military, I encourage you to embrace the suck. That's just your brain telling you that enlightenment is close. So consciously lean into that frustration and confusion. That's your sign that a breakthrough is right around the corner.

1

SELLING IS NOBLE

" Sales is
a noble
profession. "

Consider this, according to the U.S. Bureau of Labor, sales is the single largest profession in The United States. Yet, a Grass Roots study revealed that just 18% of consumers have a positive view of the sales profession. Meanwhile, more than 50% of college grads are likely to work in sales at some point in their careers.

The final kicker? Less than 3% of the 4,000 colleges in The United States have a sales program, or even teach a single sales-specific course.

That is a perfect storm. Sales currently has the most jobs, gets the most complaints, and provides employees the least education of any major profession. It's no wonder people have been programmed to have such a dim view of salespeople, they've probably encountered a lot of bad ones. This, unfortunately, has bled into salespeople's pictures of themselves. They deny themselves because they've been denied by others.

"SALES CURRENTLY HAS THE MOST JOBS, GETS THE MOST COMPLAINTS AND PROVIDES ITS EMPLOYEES THE LEAST EDUCATION OF ANY MAJOR PROFESSION."

I believe sales is the most denied job in the world next to prostitution (really). I've seen the resumes, people will go to crazy lengths to call themselves anything but a salesperson: sales consultant, product specialist, counselor, product officer, service representative, even "results achievement specialist."

I once spoke with a CEO who had a salesperson who wasn't meeting her quota. She was on the brink of getting fired because she'd spent the last 12 months developing a relationship with one prospect, who did eventually turn into a client. I noticed that her title was "relationship manager," and so I asked this CEO what her primary job duty was. He told me, "She has to sell a certain number of contracts each year to keep her job." I replied, "But you've programmed her to think she's cultivating relationships. She just spent the last 12 months on one small contract, and her focus was on building a relationship, not making a sale. And she did a great job at that. It's even in her job title. And yet, she's being paid to make sales, right? Do you see how this could create some mental dissonance?" At this, his eyes lit up, he realized at once the power of programming.

I see this all the time. This is all programming, and it's damaging to results. Sales, in my view, is the most noble profession you can pursue. It is literally the business of life improvement. But you first have to embrace it.

A sales warrior knows that sales is fundamentally a mission to improve lives, and that fact soaks into the mentality of everything they do. They realize that their mission is to bring the pride, purpose, and respect back to professional selling. And because this belief is their personal truth, their actions reflect it. They're advisors, not vendors, for their prospect's deepest needs. They want to solve their prospects' problems because they realize they're freeing them from the dungeon of ambiguity. This is the very definition of noble.

This may seem like a softer belief than the others on the surface, but it might just be the most important. When people deny their identity, or have it denied for them, it takes a severe toll on every facet of their self-image.

Think about that idea of labeling yourself as a "customer liaison", or a "relationship manager." Think about how a denied self-image influences your behaviors. That belief becomes self-fulfilling. You get paid by the sales you make, not the relationships you develop, right?

Just imagine if you went to a psychiatrist and you spent the entire hour talking, and at the end of the hour they just told you to leave without saying a word because, in their words, "eventually you'll figure it out." You'd leave that psychiatrist. They're not actually providing you any value for your time.

Sales warriors have to understand their prospects' problems, but they also have to present solutions and resolve the sale. As a sales warrior, it's your mission to lead the prospect to life improvement, and that means guiding them through the sales process. You can't do that if you label yourself as a helper. Now you're just releasing your prospects to the confusion and tyranny of their own mind.

I had a client named Jen who believed it was in her prospects' best interests to give them product information and then leave them to deliberate and make the decision to purchase, or not purchase, on their own. When I asked Jen why, Jen's positive intention was to create a welcoming environment for her prospects, but by leaving them alone, she was creating stress in her prospects, not certainty. Over time, I had to help her reframe her view of sales as a noble profession. Once she embraced her identity as a sales warrior, she was able to let go of any fears or insecurities she had about selling, and her numbers skyrocketed.

People don't have a problem with salespeople in general, they have a problem with salespeople who are boring, unhelpful, or unethical. You are the primary source of confidence, motivation, hope, and certainty for your prospects. That doesn't come from being a "relationship manager", it comes from being a sales warrior.

Stop trying to change your title, and start changing your self-image.

APPLICATION

To create a positive mental picture of sales, you have to physically see what that picture looks like to fully experience it. That's why this vision board exercise will give you a tangible benchmark for how you want to project your profession to the world.

Follow these steps to embody the reality that sales is a noble profession.

1. What comes to mind when you think of the sales profession that inspires you? What images come to mind? Think of the customers you'll be supporting, the services you'll be providing, and the life improvement you'll be leading them to.

2. Take these mental images and make them physical. Print out from websites, or cut out from magazines, the images that create a vision of the ideal sales profession in your mind's eye. Then glue these images to a poster board to create a collage of what a noble sales profession looks like to you.

3. Keep this vision board close to your desk as inspiration. Whenever you feel your view of sales waning, or feeling uncertain, call back to your vision board for strength on why sales is noble.

2

THE 4 QUESTIONS THAT WILL CHANGE YOUR LIFE

"**Every goal I set will be met.**"

When you look back at your life, I believe you'll be measured by two things: who did you become, and what did you contribute.

The reason you set goals is not to add something else to your plate, or to just have some token exercise to make you feel better for a few months before you abandon the chase for something else, the reason you set goals is to become a better version of you, and contribute as much as possible while you're on this earth.

"YOU'LL BE MEASURED BY TWO THINGS: WHO DID YOU BECOME, AND WHAT DID YOU CONTRIBUTE."

The problem we have is that the general population makes goal-setting so complicated that they just don't want to do it. Think about the gym membership cycle. On average, 80% of new gym members who join in January quit within five months. It's because their goal was either too complicated, too poorly defined, or too overwhelming. We need to simplify the process, pattern, and strategy and turn it from a to-do list into a goal, and from something you have to do into something you want to do. And that's why I developed The Four Questions to Change Your Life.

Creating a stretch goal is plan-based. You may be able to visualize yourself at the summit of the mountain, but you need to strategize the path upward first. And that's why these four questions will change everything for you:

1. What do I want to accomplish by when?
2. Why is it important to me?
3. How will I accomplish it?
4. Whose coaching do I need?

Goal-setting is at its most stressful when it's chunked up to its biggest level. That means the only thing you see is the massive goal itself. Need to hit a certain number of sales by the end of the month? Focusing on that number, and not your next move, only creates anxiety and causes you to put down your goal forever.

Instead, the purpose of these four questions is to chunk it down by clarifying the goal, setting a deadline, establishing the emotional connection to it, coming up with the steps, and listing out the external help you need. That's the mental foundation for any goal you set for the rest of your life, no matter how big or small.

Improved performance is all about increasing the consistency and effect of what you do on a daily basis. And the key to effective goal-setting is giving yourself a consistent process to follow on the smallest scope possible.

For instance, famous golfer, Arnold Palmer, always believed that his goal at the Masters tournament was to shoot a 54. He arrived at that number because if you added up his best scores on each hole over dozens of rounds, you'd arrive at a 54.

That's a great example of a stretch goal. If he focused on one hole at a time, and not the 54, he knew he could put together his best round ever.

Had Palmer set a goal for a 44, it would've been a different matter. Your subconscious will reject goals if you can't see them or experience them in your mind. That's why sales warriors with a 5% conversion rate don't set a goal for a 50% conversion rate. You might set a goal to go from 5% to 10%, then from 10% to 15%.

Once you can consistently reach each incremental goal, you raise the bar. You goal through! That's true progress, and it's the way to turn goal-setting anxiety into goal-setting achievement.

APPLICATION

Goal-setting is simple, it's just the psychology that gets in the way.

By chunking down your goal-setting to the smallest possible chunk, you're giving yourself the best chance at success. So, just take the time, answer these four questions with your biggest sales goal right now, and watch yourself become unleashed. Be sure to repeat this process with every goal you set in the future.

1. What do I want to accomplish by when?
2. Why is it important to me?
3. How will I accomplish it?
4. Whose coaching do I need?

3

THE MASTERY PYRAMID

> "I have a relentless focus on playing for mastery every day."

Every sales warrior lives and breathes mastery.

In my own life, I've seen what it looks like to be playing at different levels while working towards the same goal. But what I've found, is that I achieve my desired outcomes more easily when I'm focused on my own motivation and drowning out the noises around me. I've found that when I'm playing for mastery, nothing can stop me.

I believe the Mastery Pyramid is the most fundamental tool you can use to guide your daily progress as a sales warrior. It's a dose of objective reality, not just about where you are right now in your behaviors and beliefs, but where you want to go in the future.

Within the construct of our Consciousness Chart, the Mastery Pyramid is within the motivation level. The Mastery Pyramid is a measure of how motivated you are to achieve your goals, succeed at a high level, and continue your push to be better than you were yesterday.

The entire pyramid is cut through the middle with a critical line. This is the separator between the profitable, "above the line" employees and unprofitable "below the line" employees. Being above the line isn't just a behavioral thing either, it's a total state of mind. And at FPG, we continually assess ourselves on this concept of being "above the line" at any given moment.

For instance, if you decide to criticize someone behind their back, that's a below the line behavior. If you choose to have a tough conversation with that person, and work out your differences, that's an above the line behavior. If you choose to deny or ignore coaching, that's a below the line behavior. If you choose to demand coaching, that's an above the line behavior.

The lowest level is playing to not lose. These are people who do the bare minimum to scrape by. Their motivation is simple: they just don't want to be fired. The next level up is playing to cruise, which is the avoidance level. They're actively trying not to be noticed by others; they do their job well enough to stay under the radar but not well enough to be noticed by management. On an achievement level, they're basically running in place.

The next level up, and the final below the line consciousness, is playing to compete. This might sound like a positive thing, but playing to compete means actively competing against your peers and company as a whole. This is a high-achieving but destructive behavior, and it's the number one enemy of work cultures. Managers convince themselves the performance is worth the headache, until their culture is ripped apart from the inside. Someone at this level will minimize the successes of their peers and look to succeed at everyone else's expense. Not good.

The first above the line behavior is playing for improvement. Now you're internally motivated; your entire focus is on improving your own sales processes and results. You're not focusing on your colleagues' successes, only your own. You're not wasting any of your energy worrying about everyone else, you're dedicated to improving your own performance every single day. You're focused on getting better, and that's a profitable state of mind.

Go up one level from there, and you're playing for the challenge. Playing for the challenge is more focused progress; now you're challenging yourself, pushing your boundaries, creating new paradigms. You're taking risks and ignoring the voice in your head that's trying to talk you down. You're hungry for more, and you've made it your mission to do at least one thing every day to push you further. You're playing against your own personal best, not anyone else's.

Finally, at the top, you're playing for mastery. Mastery is about being one with your own progress as a sales warrior and living this concept of relaxed focus, and it is about helping others achieve mastery as well. Think of the scene in *The Matrix* in the hallway when Neo stops the incoming bullets and plucks one out of the air. That's mastery. That's having such a wide view of something that you can slow it down, and make it do exactly what you want.

At its core, being above the line means having something called an internal locus of control. Psychologically, this means that you don't need any external point of comparison for your own self-worth. You're playing and winning as a sales warrior on your own terms, not on anyone else's. The further up the pyramid you go, the less threatened you feel. If you're playing to not lose, everyone and everything is a threat to your success and happiness. If you're playing for mastery, you have realized that all the threats from the past were illusions.

APPLICATION

You can't truly begin your personal journey within The Mastery Pyramid without first realizing where you are within it right now. By starting from a baseline and having a real, true picture about where you are right now, you'll take the first step toward true mastery.

Follow these steps to begin that journey today.

1. Objectively place yourself on the pyramid based on where you believe you are today the majority of the time. Are you playing to not lose, and doing the bare minimum? Are you cruising, setting your sales on autopilot just hoping not to be noticed? Are you competing against your own team members or company? Or, are you above the line, playing for improvement, challenge, or even mastery?

2. Choose to take one new step every week towards the next level on the pyramid. Identify where you currently are on the pyramid, and answer the questions related to where you currently are so you can focus on moving up to the next level.

   - Playing to not lose:
     - How can you see your current situation differently?
     - What's one new way you can contribute to your team that you can put into action right now?

   - Playing to cruise:
     - What's one step you can take to turn off the autopilot?
     - It helps to gameify your sales based on your own standard. How can you beat a previous best? Chart your progress.

   - Playing to compete:
     - How can you stop seeing your teammates or company as a threat?
     - Commit to publicly celebrating your team's successes, and judging yourself only on your own successes.

   - Playing for improvement:
     - How can you make yourself even more indispensable for

your team?

- o You're already trying to improve yourself, but how can you challenge yourself even more?

- Playing for the challenge:
  - o How can you chase mastery?
  - o What's one way you can stretch yourself by helping to improve someone else? What do you need to unlearn?

- Playing for mastery:
  - o How can you make others better?
  - o Begin judging yourself not on your own successes, but on the successes of the people around you. This is a true mastery-level mindset.

3. Determine how you are going to hold yourself accountable to your new behavior. Create calendar reminders to reassess and monitor your progress.

4

YOUR PROGRAMMING MAKES YOUR SUCCESS

"I control my mindset because I control my programming."

Your mindset about yourself, and the world around you, is constantly shaped by the significant events in your life. If you've ever lost a loved one suddenly, it's more common for you to withdraw from similar relationships in the future. If you've ever been in a car accident, you might avoid certain highways or vehicles. It's the same as when a soldier witnesses the horrific scenes on a battlefield first hand, they might return home with PTSD.

Mindset through programming can be positive, too. If you're raised in a family with driven, career-focused parents, you will most likely succeed at least to the economic level you were raised. If you're continually surrounded by positive messaging after huge events or initiatives – "you're capable," "you're enough," "I believe in you" – you'll tell yourself those messages when you hit life's inevitable patches of turbulence.

Look, life doesn't always go as you plan, I'm sure you've learned that by now. There're times in your life where you lay in your bed at night wondering how in the world you got to this point. Maybe you've just been let go, or you've lost someone you love, or you're wondering how you're going to support a new baby on the way. These are major life shocks, moments that anyone would agree are hugely formational. But what about the other 99% of your life? What is that doing to your mindset, to your programming as a person?

A lot, as it turns out.

The problem is that we universally agree that major moments shape our lives, and conveniently ignore the effect of the rest. What about that small moment when you decided not to follow up on a prospect? What about those dozens of seemingly insignificant moments when you saw your boss resolve a conflict by yelling instead of talking it out? Or, when you saw that huge to-do list one day and decided to put it off until tomorrow? Or, when you went home for Thanksgiving a couple years ago, and your uncle spent an hour explaining to you why he hates salespeople?

Your brain is being programmed with every interaction, experience, and moment in your life. These things shape your mindset, and your mindset shapes your results. You can't embody the mindset of a sales warrior unless you take total control of your own programming first, and choose to reprogram yourself to become a better version of you.

You've been programmed in three distinct ways. Each of these would be an example of negative programming.

1. See. You see a peer ask a prospect, "Let me know if you have any questions" versus. asking a prospect to buy. And so going forward with all prospects, you end every conversation with, "Let me know if you have any questions."

2. Learn. You're taught by an author or speaker to wait for a buying signal before asking them to purchase, and you follow the advice.

3. Revolt. You're told to follow a new selling process that will feel uncomfortable, and decide not to use it.

And here are three examples of positive programming in action.

1. See. You see your coach consistently praise others and choose to do the same.

2. Learn. You're taught how to sell through objections successfully.

3. Revolt. You're told selling is about making friends first, and choose to make it about resolution instead.

When a customer says they don't trust most salespeople, and you verbally agree with them, that's programming. When you see a movie that depicts a salesperson as the bad guy, that's programming. When you go out on a limb to ask someone to buy, and they angrily respond with a "no," that's programming.

So, the question is, what does a sales warrior do with that? And the answer is that they start from awareness. They ask themselves one simple question: is this belief serving me well, or is holding me back?

The best way to reverse your negative programming, is to drag it out into the light. If you have role rejection as a salesperson, then don't hide from it. Confront it. Why might you have been programmed to think that way? If you believe nobody buys on the first conversation, where did that programming come from? If you believe the best way to make a sale is to make a friend, that's programming. Where did that come from? Did you see that in someone else? Was it learned? Or did a period of revolt lead to that belief?

Examining your programming is a process, but it starts with awareness. Once you start eliminating the negative programming you've experienced and replace it with something that aligns you with your mission as a sales warrior, you've taken another step forward on your journey.

APPLICATION

Coming to terms with your own programming is the first step on the journey. Take some time and go back through your own past timeline, and
give yourself the gift of awareness. Make sure you're honest with yourself
about the situations in your life that have programmed you to think or behave in a specific way.

Follow these steps to begin reprogramming yourself.

1. From your past, list out three ways you've been negatively programmed as it relates to your sales career. Choose one each from
   the see, learn, and revolt categories. Moving forward, commit to
   overturning this negative programming whenever you see it arise.

2. From your past, list out three ways you've been positively programmed as it relates to your sales career. Choose one each from
   the see, learn, and revolt categories. Moving forward, commit to
   using this positive programming to fuel your success.

3. Repeat this process often to build on your positive programming
   around your sales career and remove your negative programming.

5

P = K - L

" I achieve maximum performance by adding more knowledge and removing my leashes. "

I believe all achievement in your life boils down to one simple-to-understand formula.

Performance = Knowledge – Leashes

Let me unpack this for you. Your performance is nothing more than your results. It's what you end up with at the end of the day. Knowledge, is what you know to do as a salesperson. These are the strategies, processes, and past learnings you've incorporated into your daily behaviors. The leashes are anything inside you that keep you from acting on the beneficial knowledge you've acquired. So if you know an award-winning sales process, but you have leashes and don't believe it will work, your leashes are holding back your knowledge, and therefore your performance.

And there are 4 types of knowledge that you need to acquire in order to remove any leashes you may have.

The first is your **brand**. Your brand messaging is what makes you unique and unrivaled as a company. It's vital that you don't just know that branding; you must own it to truly sell it.

The second is your **product**. The products, features and benefits you sell are what give your company the unique selling position it currently occupies. Your success, and the success of your company, often depends on how well you can sell your products based upon the knowledge you possess.

The third is **finance**. Top sales warriors know the financial side of their products inside and out. You can comfortably and simply explain the financing and payment plan options as well as the benefits and the return on investment your prospects will get when they purchase with you.

The last type of knowledge is **selling skill**. The most effective selling is 80% process-driven science and 20% individual art. That means having a defined, science-based process that allows you to sell to any prospect, in any situation.

So that's your knowledge. But if you want maximum performance, you can't just know how to do something, you also have to work on removing your leashes. Your leashes are the mental roadblocks that stop you from following your process. There are four types of leashes you're fighting every day.

1. Self-image
Your self-image as a sales warrior represents your internal beliefs about yourself and your capabilities. For example, if you say to yourself, "I'm not a talented enough salesperson to earn a six-figure income."

2. Stories

A story is an assumption based on external circumstances that may, or may not be, true. For example, if you say "people don't buy the kinds of products that I sell in a down economy."

3. Reluctances

A reluctance is a fear of selling in a certain situation, or to a certain type of person. For example, a fear of closing sales over the phone or a fear of selling to a high net worth individual.

4. Rules

Rules are what you need to see, feel, or hear in order to have permission to engage with your prospect. For example, if you say, "I never ask for the close until at least the third conversation."

The key is to move through each one. Start with your self-image; build up your belief in yourself and your abilities. Then, conquer your stories, reluctances, and the limiting rules you have.

We'll unpack those individual leashes more in the next few chapters, but for now, let's focus on the performance formula itself.

The performance you get on a daily basis is equal to the amount of knowledge you have, minus the number of leashes you have. So, it follows that true sales warriors are constantly focused on two things: adding knowledge and removing leashes. And both are a never-ending quest to find ultimate performance.

The good news is that you can take steps to increase your knowledge every single day. You can read more books, watch TED Talks, role play selling situations with your peers, or sign up for an FPG training program. The knowledge you have is the behavioral cornerstone of your success as a sales warrior. And the sales warrior mindset, firmly believes that the true quest for knowledge never stops.

One thing that *will* stop your quest for performance, are unchecked leashes. These are the negative internal voices that constrain you from reaching your goals and improving on your performance from the day before.

Just think about it mathematically, if your leashes outweigh your knowledge, then your performance score will be a negative. If your knowledge is greater than your leashes, then you'll get a positive performance score. I believe that gameifying anything is a great way to create self-motivation, and it's the same with the performance score. How can you take steps to increase your sales knowledge while simultaneously decreasing your leashes? That's how you reach peak performance.

I came up with this performance formula because I saw leashes holding people back everywhere I looked. Nothing is more frustrating than seeing someone with the innate ability to succeed held back by leashes they're not being coached to break.

Years ago, when I first started my training career, I figured this out the hard way. I'd personally trained a client for months solely to give him more knowledge in an effort to help him sell more. I struggled with how I could teach him all this knowledge, only to see it never implemented in the end. The answer finally came. He couldn't follow through because of his leashes. He didn't need any more knowledge, he needed his leashes removed. That's when I realized the training industry needed a shakeup, and it was going to start with me.

The heart of behavior change is removing your own leashes so you can become a sales warrior. So what does that mean for you? Maybe that's releasing your fear around asking for the sale. Maybe it's your tendency to run from coaching.

Whatever it is, it's time to confront those leashes and eliminate them.

APPLICATION

Leashes are anything that hold you back from becoming the sales warrior you were born to be. Follow this leash turnaround process – my adaptation of Byron Katie's *The Work* – to examine, explore, and minimize the leashes you have today.

1. Write a list of any negative feelings, thoughts, or ideas you have about yourself as a salesperson or about sales in general.

2. For each thing on this list follow this unleashing process. Ask yourself these questions:

   - Is this a fact? If so, what's the evidence?
   - How do you feel when you believe this thought?
   - How do you react when you believe this thought?
   - What happens when you believe this thought?
   - Why physical sensations arise when you believe this thought?
   - Who would you be without this thought?
   - What is the opposite of this belief.
   - What is the evidence that supports this new truth?

3. Embrace this new thought. If your initial belief was, "I don't have enough time to be successful," then your new belief is, "I have all the time I need to be successful." This is your new truth. Write this new unleashing belief on 3 index cards. Keep one in your house, one in your car, and one at work. For the next 30 days, collect evidence to support this thought.

6

LEASH #1: SELF-IMAGE

"My self-image contributes to my success."

Your self-image as a sales warrior represents your internal beliefs about yourself. The most common problem with self-image, not just in sales warriors, but in the human race, is that it too often gets mixed up between what you believe about yourself, and what your brain says others believe about you.

I want you to think about a time in your life when you didn't get what you wanted, and your self-esteem shot down. Maybe it was a college rejection letter, or a bad breakup, or maybe you got passed up for a big promotion.

to do something, you can. There's no one stopping you except you—and your circumstances don't hold you back, only the leashes you create with your own self-image.

Right now, you hold an image of yourself in your mind. This image is a summary of all your past programming: your past behaviors, learnings, successes, setbacks. According to famed creator of Psycho-Cybernetics Maxwell Maltz, this creates two parallel realities for you right now.

1. You act, behave, and feel in accordance with the self-image you have of yourself, and you don't deviate from it.
2. Your self-image can be changed.

Maltz was a plastic surgeon, and when he operated on his patients, he noticed that for some, the physical improvement didn't improve their mental self-image. One woman walked in wanting her broken nose fixed because it was hurting her self-image. However, when she looked in the mirror after he removed the bandages, she still felt broken. Her inner reality hadn't changed. She still felt scarred and shattered, even though her nose was fixed. He called this "*The Stranger Within*," because so often we don't even identify with ourselves when we really examine our warped self-image.

We've seen examples like this one all across our culture. Young Hollywood stars start their careers wide-eyed and fresh-faced, but their self-image isn't strong enough to handle the external pressure, and so they crack. An athlete suffers a meltdown during a game, and their self-image crumbles. It's because their self-image was defined by their critics' opinions and outside circumstances.

Just the same, I believe that every salesperson wakes up every day with a certain dollar sign in their head, and they will do anything they can to make that dollar sign come true. This is completely self-image related. If you believe you're worth $55,000, then your subconscious self-image will take over and you'll do the things it takes to earn $55,000. If you believe you're worth three times that number? Then your behavior patterns completely change. You begin studying and modeling the most successful people and altering your goals to achieve what you want to achieve. Everything changes.

"YOUR SELF-IMAGE CAN BE CHANGED."

Famed speaker and author, Dr. Wayne Dyer, said something so profound that I've used this one quote to guide my own self-image: "When you change the way you look at things, the things you look at change."

So, if you want to change your own self-image, you have to change the things you look at. An important way to do this is to alter your focus. Your negative self-image as a salesperson is fed by all kinds of past programming: lost sales, jobs that didn't work out, monetary setbacks. Those are all circumstantial factors.

Instead, choose gratitude. Shape your self-image into what *you* want it to be by mentally channeling success. What did you do to move that one sale forward last week? How did you give yourself a pay raise in the past? What can you do to improve upon that? How can you use your past success to solidify future successes?

Your own self-image can be a tyrant, but you can give yourself the gift of freedom by taking control of it and creating your own image.

Whatever your own negative beliefs about your identity as a salesperson are, you have the power to reverse them. All it takes is a decision.

APPLICATION

People with a positive self-image are able to live their life by those images and take pride in their abilities and accomplishments. Having a positive self-image doesn't mean tricking yourself into believing you are flawless, but it means knowing your positive qualities and using them to change the undesired qualities.

So, here's how you can improve your self-image so you can start living the life you are worth.

1. What dollar amount do you believe you're worth as a salesperson?

2. Write down the average income you've earned in the last three years of your career.

3. Notice the gap between what your conscious mind believes you're worth, what you've actually earned, versus what your subconscious mind believes you're worth, what you answered in question one. If the numbers are different, then your inner "thermostat" is regulating your income and readjusting your income to match what you believe subconsciously is your worth.

4. Commit to closing the gap. Larry Page, the former CEO of Google, once said that he wanted everyone at Google to have a 50% failure rate with at least half of their goals. This pushed them to close the gap between what they earned, and what they're truly worth.

How can you increase the failure rate of your goals to earn what you're truly worth?

7

LEASH #2: STORIES

> "I control the stories I tell myself about my circumstances."

Your mind is constantly working, with or without your permission. It's constantly filling your conscious, and subconscious, with stories about the world around you. And those stories, unfortunately, are often both fictional and harmful. When told consistently, those fictional stories become leashes that hinder your growth and limit your performance.

It's just a truth that salespeople with fewer external stories around prospects and their circumstances will have fewer leashes, carry fewer assumptions, and have a stronger ability to achieve. So your goal as a sales warrior, is to develop what I call your "story filter." This is a cultivated ability to get rid of the stories about your circumstances that hold you back, and only internalize the stories you know to be true or beneficial. And that means constantly asking yourself these three questions on a daily basis.

1. Is this story true? If so, how do I know?

2. Is this story beneficial to me?

3. How can I use this story in a positive way?

Imagine you're at work, and your coach is short with you all day. You ask questions and you get short replies. You're filling up your coffee cup in the break room and you get a cold shoulder. The story you tell yourself in that moment is that your boss is mad at you, that you've done something wrong, and if you allow the story to go to its furthest extreme, that your employment status is up in the air.

These are stories you've told yourself. They're fictitious, and they create a defensive, anxious posture. In reality, your coach is just as likely to have just gotten bad news that morning. It more than likely has nothing to do with you. This is where communication is key. Before you create a story about something, you must verify its truth before you manifest it as your own reality. Otherwise you're filling your head with performance-destroying illusions.

In the bestselling book, *A Course in Miracles*, it says, "whenever you become defensive about anything, know that you have identified with an illusion."

That's what happens when we tell ourselves stories about the world around us. And sales warriors know that one of the keys to becoming unleashed is to liberate yourself from those debilitating stories

The stories salespeople tell themselves about prospects, the economy, the competition, their product, and the price vary, but they're rarely true. If a prospect has their arms crossed, the story might read, "They're not happy with me or my product, I need to back off." The problem is, you don't know that to be true, which becomes a huge problem when you base your entire selling message off of it.

There's no question these stories come from somewhere, but they rarely spring from the root cause of what the true story actually is. It may feel like your boss is purposely neglecting you, but they might just not have the resources to know how to handle your problem. It may feel like your prospects don't want to be asked to purchase on the first conversation, but that may indicate your own discomfort more than anything else.

The bottom line is that the stories we tell ourselves about our circumstances leash our behaviors. If you've internalized a story, it can be difficult to get rid of without the proper tools.

Your tendency to tell yourself success-crippling stories is an important leash to reverse, because it feeds entirely off illusion. The story has to be fought the moment it arrives, otherwise, it implants itself into your consciousness and becomes part of your assumed reality.

So, your goal is to become conscious of the stories your brain feeds you. Take control of the process, and this is how you do it.

APPLICATION

The stories you tell yourself create your map for the world around you. By controlling those stories, you create a more accurate map of the world that allows you to have more influence and control over your messaging.

1. Check the boxes that directly apply to the stories you tell yourself about your circumstances.

   ☐ I know my prospect is not engaged when they aren't smiling.

   ☐ I know my prospect likes what I'm selling when they ask questions.

   ☐ I know my prospect wants to be sold when their body language tells me they want to be sold.

   ☐ I know my prospect has a better chance of buying from me when they've already heard about my product or service.

   ☐ Prospects don't want to be closed on the first conversation.

   ☐ My prospects don't want me to initiate conversation.

   ☐ My prospects will tell me when they're ready to buy.

2. Notice any items you checked off. These are now your focus as you seek to remove rules from your selling process. Commit to the opposite belief (i.e. "My prospect's facial expressions have no bearing on their interest in my product or service") and make this your new truth.

3. As you go, continue to notice the rules you impose on your sales, and always make the opposite freeing leash your new truth.

8

LEASH #3: RELUCTANCES

"My reluctances were learned, so they can be unlearned."

You're at work, nervously tapping your fingers on your desk, darting your eyes anxiously between your phone and your lengthy cold call list. The more you do this, the more anxious you feel, and the more the barrier between your current state and action grows. Finally, you decide to put off the task and do some organizational work in your CRM.

This is an example of what's called a reluctance, specifically telephobia, which is the fear of selling over the phone. A reluctance is any mental hesitancy that causes you to stop your own sale. And no matter who you are, you have some area of reluctance. The key is identifying what they are so you can do something about it.

The Sales Preference Questionnaire, published by The Behavioral Sciences Research Press, is a game-changing reluctance assessment we use with all of our clients, and it measures the key mental reluctances salespeople have. The purpose in identifying Call Reluctance* is to balance out your performance formula. Just as you're increasing your knowledge by planting more resources, it's equally important to tend to your mental garden by pulling your mental leashes like weeds. And your reluctances are one of the four types.

In a recent study done within an insurance agency, the annual cost of call reluctance or sales reluctance was over $5 million. In another study among financial service agents, those employees with lower levels of call reluctance recorded over twice as much prospecting activity compared to those with higher levels. And in another study among real estate agents, agents who had higher sales reluctance had over $4,000 less in sales commissions per month and over $53,000 per year. In other words, these reluctances determine a lot about your results.

Here are the six most statistically common reluctances salespeople deal with on a daily basis. You might see yourself in one or several of these, but don't panic. People are not their reluctances. You weren't born with reluctances. You were programmed to have them; from the media, parents, experiences, sales managers, and even sales trainers.

1. **Yielder.** The fear of appearing too pushy, intrusive or high pressure, which limits asking for the sale or handling objections.

2. **Over-Preparer.** The tendency to spend too much time preparing what to say and how to say it, and too little time prospecting for people to give their presentations to. In short, it's the tendency to over-analyze and under-act.

---

3. **Arranging payment.** This is related to how people behave when they need to close a deal. It's the generalized fear that they will somehow jeopardize the sale during the arranging payment phase.

4. **Telephobia.** The belief that people buy in person, not over the phone, which limits effectiveness in making and being proactive on prospecting calls.

5. **Referral Aversion.** The belief that asking for referrals will threaten a just-closed sale, damage delicate rapport with their current customers, or appear to be exploiting the relationship.

6. **Social Self-Consciousness.** This is where you are intimidated by up-market clientele, meaning you are reluctant to sell to people who are older, more educated, or wealthier than you are.

People aren't born with these reluctances. A salesperson with referral aversion might've been taught by some experience that asking for referrals will endanger the sale. An over-preparer might've had a parent who instilled in them a belief that you can never spend too much time preparing for something. All those experiences contribute to those reluctances.

But one thing that definitely doesn't contribute to those reluctances? Your genetics. Who you are.

My first job out of college was at a major financial firm, and I remember clear as day one of the first things my boss told me: "Make sure there's never a single question about the stock market you can't answer on a daily basis." His positive intention behind that idea was great. He wanted me to be prepared. But the actual result of that programming was the installation of an over-preparer leash that took me years to overcome.

I would start every day at 5:30 a.m. and spend an hour and a half reading the Wall Street Journal from cover to cover, searching out every shred of investment business news to satisfy my new over-preparer reluctance. Did I need to spend eight hours every week reading? Or could I have spent less time reading and more time on the phone, selling to prospects?

It created a small voice of fear in my head that gradually grew to a roar. I kept telling myself, "Jason, you don't have enough information to act yet.

Keep reading." I was constantly worried that my prospects would find me out, would ask me a question I couldn't answer and embarrass me. That's a reluctance in action, and it was devastating to my results.

Someone with telephobia tendencies could easily have been programmed by a negative experience over the phone. I know salespeople who worked in call centers as their first job in sales, and they were programmed negatively by experience after experience of hang-ups, rude responses, and prospects who continually let it ring to voicemail. Over time, they're programmed to believe that nobody wants to be sold on the phone. And that reluctance ends up inhibiting their results for the rest of their career.

The good news? You learned your reluctances, which means you can also unlearn them. Your reluctances are not a sign of your condition as a person, they're just a sign of your current state of mind.

And as you already know, you can change your state of mind. All it takes is a decision.

APPLICATION

Removing your reluctances is a three-part process, no matter what it is. Whenever you feel those tendencies bubbling up to the surface, make this your immediate reaction.

1. **Recognize your positive intention.** For instance, if you have yielder tendencies, which is the fear of being too pushy, your positive intention might be to help and respect your prospect by giving them space to discuss their needs and determine what they want.

2. **Change your perspective to see that your current process, pattern and strategy isn't helping you achieve your positive intention.** By yielding to the prospect, you're releasing them to an ambiguous state they're not prepared to handle. Therefore, you're not helping them.

3. **Redirect to a new behavior that fulfills your positive intention.** Instead of yielding, I will actually *give* my prospect the best possible experience by leaning into my discomfort and actively leading them through the sales process, which will help them.

This is a powerful way to reframe your mindset to take whatever reluctance you have and diminish it until it's no longer a fear. And the more you follow this process, the more you'll see your reluctances shrink. To take an SPQ and get your own personalized report, contact us at **sales@FPG.com**.

9

LEASH #4: RULES

"I always have permission to engage with my prospects."

I believe that the quality of your life is equal to the number of rules you have. Think about the dating world. We all know someone who has a laundry list of requirements for their significant other: must love dogs, must be physically fit, must have a certain political affiliation, must be a teacher, must have a certain hair color.

It's no surprise that the more rules you have, the more single you are.

This doesn't just apply to the world of dating. It's a universal truth. If you go into a car-buying situation with 400 hard rules for your car, you probably aren't walking out with a car that day. If you expect someone to act according to a long list of rules you've set, and they violate your self-imposed rules, then you'll inevitably be disappointed in them.

This doesn't mean you don't get what you want, it just means you remove the rules you've created for yourself so you can see the bigger picture and get exactly what you *need*.

In a selling sense, rules are what you need to see, hear, or feel in order to have permission to engage with your prospect.

As a salesperson, these rules take a number of forms. Here are a few examples of common rules I've seen salespeople use as an excuse for why they did things a certain way.

1. "I only go for the close if they've said they want to buy from us."
2. "I only follow up three times because anything more than that is annoying."
3. "I only decide to sell to people who express an interest in what we sell."
4. "The right time to ask for the sale is after the third conversation."

Every one of these is an example of a rule influenced by programming. Maybe that salesperson made a sale one time after the third conversation and then created a rule around it, or, they successfully sold a prospect who showed positive body language once and created a rule around that experience. This is how the brain naturally fills in the blanks for you.

"FREEDOM AND RULES DON'T MIX."

We've talked a lot about freedom as it relates to your leashes, and that's for a reason. The number one thing humans desire in life is freedom. A recent three-university study found that the reason people want power in life, isn't because they want control, it's because they want freedom. They want freedom to make their own choices, the freedom to decide their fate, the freedom to create their own journey.

Freedom and rules don't mix. The more mental rules you add onto your life, whether consciously or unconsciously, the less freedom you have to choose your own path. The rules you create are the mental handcuffs that keep you from achieving your goals. Logically, you need to decrease the number of rules you have in order to increase your own personal capacity for freedom.

Richard Tiller, award-winning sales coach and author, tells a great story of a salesperson he coached named Brad, who was tripping over a sales rule. Brad would only close people when they seemed obviously interested in buying, and that never happened on the first interaction. He wasn't making his quota, and since he believed nobody wanted to buy that soon, he never tried to close them that soon.

So Richard made a calculated guess. He asked Brad, "I'd bet you're pretty meticulous when you make buying decisions. You start with 10 items, then narrow to 5, then narrow to 3, then choose which is best, right?" Brad responded, "Of course! How else would someone be able to make an informed decision?"

Here was the problem. Brad was so set in his own rule that he sold to his prospects as if he was selling to himself. So Richard gave Brad an assignment: sell to your prospects as though you were selling to someone who *didn't* need all that time and energy to make a buying decision. Sell to them as though they wanted to make a purchase that very day.

When Richard checked in with Brad three months later, he'd quadrupled his sales. He didn't set out to change his process, he just changed his perspective around his rule, instead of limitations, he saw possibilities. He eliminated his rule.

A sales warrior has one primary rule around selling: their prospect is breathing. Other than that, a sales warrior isn't handcuffed by the rules they've created for themselves. They believe everyone wants to be sold to. They believe there is no wrong time to ask for the sale. They believe no external source is keeping them from selling more. And that's because they have no rules beyond three simple criteria.

1. Is it legal?

2. Is it moral?

3. Is it ethical?

So going forward, stay within these criteria, and you'll break leashes every single day.

APPLICATION

The first step to letting go of the rules you have about selling, is knowing what they are. Once you're aware of these rules, you can consciously take steps to remove them from your life. Follow these four steps by answering the following questions to identify your rules.

1. I could sell more if only...
2. How do you decide if someone wants to be sold to?
3. When is generally the right time to ask for the close?

Next, take each answer through a counter-example template:

"Was there ever a time when _____ didn't_____?"

4. Then answer those yourself to see the result. If you don't know of anyone personally, search your scenario to find someone who successfully sold in that situation.

Example: "I could sell more if only the price was lower," turns into, "Was there ever a time when lowering the price didn't matter?" Then answer with a time when you sold, or know of someone who sold, without lowering the price.

Example: "I sell only if all decision-makers are present," turns into "Was there ever a time when the lack of every decision-maker didn't stop someone from making the sale?" Then answer with a time when a lack of a decision-maker didn't prevent you or someone you know of making a sale.

10

THE 6 HUMAN NEEDS

> "I fulfill my 6 Human Needs."

Every human being is on a never-ending quest to fulfill their 6 Human Needs. The more needs you fill, the closer you get to crushing your goals. It's really that simple.

The 6 Human Needs is a popular concept developed by Tony Robbins, and it's a revised variant of Abraham Maslow's hierarchy of needs. In my experience, the level of your motivation to achieve your goals is directly related to your ability to tie that goal to your 6 Human Needs. When you can fulfill three human needs, you'll become addicted to your goal. When you can fulfill all six? That's called a super-addiction, and it's that kind of motivation that built empires like Apple and Microsoft.

Focus on keeping these needs filled in every area of your life, and you'll have all the motivation you need to achieve any goal you set in your life, big or small.

1. **Certainty**

    When it comes to certainty, we all need safety in life. When certainty is lost, all is lost. Certainty is the foundational need. How will your goal increase your certainty in areas like your finances, your family, or your job?

2. **Variety**

    If you don't have enough variety in your life, you'll become incredibly bored. But if you have too much variety in your life, you'll become overwhelmed. Think of variety like the spice of life. It's the need for excitement, adventure and surprise. How will your goal increase your variety in areas like vacations, job roles or daily tasks?

3. **Significance**

    Every single one of us wants to feel like we matter. We want to feel like we're wanted in life. Significance is the need to be wanted, to have meaning, and to have a sense of importance in life. How will your goal increase your significance within your job and with the people around you?

4. **Love & Connection**

    This is about finding love and connecting with others, whether that's family, friends, or colleagues. Humans are inherently social beings, and we all want to have that tribe we can connect with. How does your goal increase your love and connection with your peers at work, and with your friends and family in your personal life?

5. **Growth**

    This is feeling like you're growing every day. People have an inner desire for growth, and when you can connect with your need to be better than you were yesterday, that's when you know you're improving your life. How will your goal increase your ability to grow and improve yourself?

6. **Contribution**

Contribution means that you want to contribute to other people in the world. You'd never want to just roll with the motions without purpose, you want to give back and use your abilities to make the world a better place. How will your goal allow you to contribute more to everyone in your life?

The reality is that every human being needs each of these needs to feel truly fulfilled, but everyone's 1-6 ranking is different. Some people may need variety more than anything else, but for others, it may be growth. No matter which is your top need, every single one matters.

Think about any relationship you've ever had. Whether you realized it at the time or not, the better the relationship, the more needs were being met.

A marriage that goes the distance provides **certainty** because both partners feel safe and comfortable around each other. It provides **variety** because they get out of their daily routine every so often and keep the relationship fresh and new, like it was at the beginning. It gives you **significance** because your partner builds you up and makes you feel big. It provides **love and connection** because you feel deeply seen by that person, inside and out. It gives you **growth** because you're both spurring each other on to be better versions of yourselves. And it gives you **contribution**, because you both feel like you're equally contributing to the success of the other.

If you were to diagnose every failed relationship in history, you could directly trace it back to multiple of these needs not being met. I'm sure you recognize how relationships that didn't serve you failed to meet some (or all) of these needs as well.

It's the same in every facet of our lives; at work, spiritually, with friends and family, within our culture. If you don't feel as though your human needs are being met, it's time to make a change and find something that makes you feel whole.

Now that you know your goal after going through The 4 Questions to Change Your Life, apply your human needs. How will that goal fulfill all six? Once you can answer that, you'll understand the power of our Goal Addiction˙ program that we provide for our clients. It gives you all the motivation you need and builds you into an unstoppable goal-achieving machine.

The first step of that journey is recognition. You deserve to have every one of your 6 Human Needs met in your life. Because once you become intentional about that, you'll find you're living the abundant life you were created for.

APPLICATION

Knowing your own 6 Human Needs hierarchy is your first step to fulfilling them in every area of your life.

1. Write down the biggest goal you have in your life right now. It could be anything, from sending your family on a vacation, to doubling your sales in the next 12 months.

2. Copy down each of the 6 Human Needs, and then write out one way your goal will help you meet that particular human need in your own life.

3. Build out this list over time so you can develop a super-addiction to your goal. Repeat the process for any goal you set.

11

LEARN, UNLEARN, REPEAT

"Because I can learn negative habits, I can unlearn them."

I want you to imagine a clock in your mind's eye. That clock is a metaphor for your entire professional journey.

You start your career at 12:00, and for the next three hours you're in what's called the "learning zone." This is where your brain acts like a sponge for new information. You're actively seeking improvement, challenge, and mastery. You're asking questions, and your ego is comparatively small in relation to the goals you're trying to accomplish. Everything seems possible in these three hours.

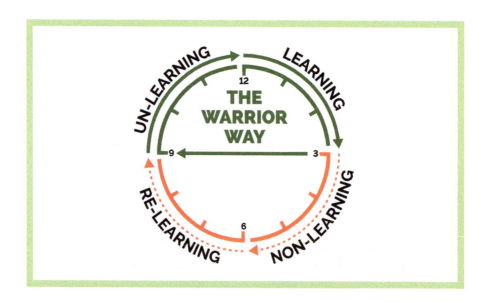

Then you hit 3:00, and your ego takes over. This is where you begin telling yourself, "I have arrived." You've achieved success, you've used your time in the learning zone wisely, and you're now in a comfortable place. At the same time, the economy is changing, the environment is changing, and you're not. You've decided to stay in the same place. This is what's called the "non-learning zone."

"I AM THE PROBLEM AND I AM ALSO THE SOLUTION."

Then you hit 6:00, and you have to make a tough decision. Circumstances changed so much in relation to how little you've changed that you hit a wall. You do one of two things: you either break down, or you break through. The deciding factor is your level of ownership. If you respond, "It's not my fault, it's the circumstances around me," then you'll go bankrupt and flame out.

But if you respond,"It's been me all along. I am the problem and I am also the solution," then you'll break through. That's the difference.

Now you're in the "relearning zone" from 6:00-9:00. This is when you hear people say, "I'm going back to the basics." They're returning to things they picked up in the learning zone and reapplying them to their life.

When you get to 9:00, the final fourth of the clock is called the "unlearning zone." This part is key. This is where you fully realize that life is about unlearning the leashes you have, as much as it's about learning new strategies to make yourself better.

The sales warrior spends the entirety of their time and energy in the learning and unlearning zones. They never tell themselves they've arrived, because they know that internal ideology kicks off a vicious cycle of breakdown. Their entire goal throughout this process is to learn something, then shift over and unlearn the leashes keeping them from executing that concept 100% of the time.

You have to embrace change and new knowledge, or you'll be left behind.

My first exposure to speaking in front of others was in the academic world, and so my professional speaking style when I first started my career was extremely strait-laced. In other words, I spoke to every audience like a professor. That served me extremely well at that moment in time, but I recognized that if I wanted to realize my goal of becoming a sought-after conference keynote speaker, I needed more energy. I needed more charisma. I just needed more.

I realized I had to unlearn the style that had served me in the past and learn a more emotionally engaging style from my new speaking coach, Steve Siebold. In other words, I had to start over on the clock. It was a process, but I now speak in front of billion-dollar companies and do more than 90 speaking events every year. It goes without saying that I'm in a much better place in my career because of it.

In one scene in *Star Wars: The Empire Strikes Back*, Luke Skywalker is struggling to lift his ship out of the swamp using the mysterious Force. Luke fails to pull it out of the muck, turns to Yoda and says in exasperation, "Moving stones around is one thing, but this is totally different."

Yoda's response: "No. No different. Only different in your mind. You must unlearn what you have learned."

What Yoda is saying, is that Luke's mind was so wrapped up in the difficulty of the task that he couldn't see the possibility. He was still living in his breakdown state. He had to *unlearn* the impossibility of the task, so he could *learn* Yoda's strategies to create his own success. Just the same, your success is equal to your ability to unlearn the things that hold you back from achieving what you want to achieve.

APPLICATION

What do you need to learn and unlearn?

1. Identify where you are on the clock right now. If you're in the non-learning zone, or the relearning zone, commit to changing your strategy to get back into the learning, or unlearning zone, immediately. Your awareness around this reality will help you avoid the 6:00 breakdown.

2. Identify the biggest thing you need to learn right now, as it relates to your sales goals. What's one thing you don't know right now that you feel would help you achieve success? Then commit to diving deep, submitting yourself to the process, and learning.

3. Identify the biggest leash or hurdle holding you back from achieving that goal. Once you've gone through the learning process, write out three specific leashes, or areas you need to unlearn, in order to achieve that goal.

4. Come up with positive affirmation statements to counter the negative beliefs you want to unlearn. For example, if your programming tells you a selling process is too robotic, unlearn that by countering with, "A selling process gives me the best chance to meet my sales goal."

5. Repeat these affirmation statements as often as possible until you achieve your goal.

12

HOW STRONG IS YOUR ME?

> " My self-image is stronger than the image the world gives me. "

Your "me" is your inner sense of self that dictates every single one of your behaviors. If you want to think about it a different way, your "me" is the bones to your skeleton. Imagine your body without your bones. Pretty horrific, right?

Think about it this way. How are you supposed to strengthen everything around your life if you don't start with your own self-image? Applying the rest of these beliefs without having a strong "me" is the equivalent of living in a boneless body.

One overarching theme of the strategies you'll find in this book is to strengthen your internal "me." When I ask people how strong their "me" is, they always tend to get a little uncomfortable. As a society, we tend to attach the concept of having a strong sense of self to having an inflated ego. But ego and sense of self are two entirely different things.

Your ego is a mask of your outer confidence. It's not who you are, it's merely a behavior you project. Your sense of self, or your "me," is your inner security. This is your internal state of being. Your "me" is your inner confidence that's filled with the stories you tell yourself about your own worthiness and capability. Your inner stories need to be louder than the stories coming from the outside. Think about the fan following of a celebrity, for instance. We see it all the time. When a person's "me" is weaker than their culture, they'll pour all of their identity into one celebrity, or cultural figurehead, that they connect with.

When that celebrity inevitably does something that lets them down, because they're human, that identity is fractured. This is the genesis of lash-out behaviors like nasty social media comments. A celebrity makes a mistake, and social media outlets blow up with angry followers attacking that celebrity. A strong, healthy "me" might debate an issue, but they'll never degrade someone else. That's a weak "me" problem.

The same thing happens with destructive cults. They're filled with people who've been programmed to have incredibly weak "me's." These cult members become consumed by the cult, and their "me" becomes so weak and feeble that their personal identity becomes the identity of the cult leader. Investigations of cults show that they suppress identities of members to steer behavior, something that someone with a strong "me" couldn't allow.

What matters most in the context of your "me", is where it's stopping. This is what the weakest "me" looks like.

In this case, the "me" is consumed by everything around them. Here's what a strong "me" looks like.

In this case, the "me" is the strongest circle. This doesn't mean a person is bigger than their family or culture or religion, but it does mean their inner story matches the outer circumstances. For instance, a religious person who decides to change churches because they don't align with the theology, has a mighty "me." They realize their outer circumstances don't match their inner identity. Someone who stops watching a TV show because it doesn't line up with their values has a strong "me." Someone who decides to leave their old friends because their values no longer match up has a strong "me." Again, they realize their outer circumstances don't match their inner identity.

It's important to recognize that a strong "me" is anything that's in alignment with your own truth, your own heart, and your own spirit. I'm a firm believer in demanding and submitting to coaching, so a strong "me" sometimes looks like listening and learning, but it's *always* aligned with a better version of you.

In short, people form and shape their inner identity first, and measure the outer circumstances against it. They tap into the "me" they were created to be, not the "me" their culture and programming creates them to be. They don't start with the outer circumstances and then come up with an inner identity that matches the world's model, because that makes for an incredibly weak "me."

Strengthening your "me" as a sales warrior is a gradual process. It doesn't happen overnight, but it's vitally essential that it happens. It's about recognizing how strong you feel around peers, coworkers, bosses, family, and all those vital areas in your life that require so much of us, every day of our lives. Being strong in those areas is the foundation of an unleashed life.

The purpose of this book is to help you become aware of your "me" and, step by step, create a stronger sense of self and mental fortitude. The great news for you is that all of these strategies will make you a better version of you. Every single one. Maybe some are more applicable than others from one moment to the next, but you'll be able to use each one to build yourself up over the course of your life.

One of my favorite quotes comes from Ayn Rand's book, *Atlas Shrugged*.

"I SWEAR BY MY LIFE AND MY LOVE OF IT THAT I WILL NEVER LIVE FOR THE SAKE OF ANOTHER MAN, NOR ASK ANOTHER MAN TO LIVE FOR MINE."

That's an awesome picture for what a strong "me" really looks like. It shows that you are so in alignment with your own truth and your own sense of self, that you don't need the approval of others to be who you truly are. You know your truth, and you live it every day.

Maybe not all of these beliefs will resonate with you right now, that's perfectly natural, but always keep in mind that this is a book for your journey. It's a mental guidebook to hold with you to strengthen your "me" all along the way.

The key is not to let others' model for the world become more powerful than the model you want to create for your own life. That, above everything else, is why your "me" must be stronger than anything else.

APPLICATION

You already have areas in your life where your "me" is currently strong. You've put in the time to create mental strength in that area by growing, learning, and adapting. For instance, if your "me" is strong around your family, then you've done the work to get it to that point.

Your first step to strengthening your "me" in areas where it isn't currently strong, is recognizing what you already do to create a strong sense of self in other areas. Follow these steps to strengthen your "me" in every area of your life.

1. Find an area where your "me" is already strong. This is anywhere you feel most fully confident, assured, and yourself. Choose from this list: Peers, Boss, Friends, Prospects, Family, Culture.

2. List out the resources in that area you've used to strengthen your own inner "me" in one area where you're already strongest. List out 5 ways you've been able to be successful in cultivating a strong "me" in that area. This could be anything from setting boundaries, to positive reinforcing self-talk.

3. Borrow those resources in areas you want your "me" to be stronger. If you find your "me" is small with your prospects but strong with your family, use the family resources you've listed (i.e. confidence or assertive communication) and commit to bringing those forward with your prospects.

4. Commit to engaging with this process over time, and practice consistency. Continually identify and bring forth resources from areas where you're already strong to round out your "me" in all areas.

13

REINVENT YOUR AUTHENTICITY

"My true authentic self is my growing self, my improving self, my learning self, my uncomfortable self."

Our authenticity is found as we grow closer to the "me" we were created to be. I once heard a story about the creation of a statue. When the sculptor was finished creating this work of art, he was approached by a young girl who asked him, "How did you create such a beautiful statue?" He replied, "I did not create the beauty. It was always part of the stone. I simply chipped away at the edges to reveal the beauty within."

We're a lot like that statue. Everything you need to be successful is within you. You just need to chip away at the edges to reveal the greatness within. You need to call out that greatness within yourself. As we continue to learn, grow, and stretch ourselves, we slowly chip away at the programming that's been concealing our unrealized ability.

You've probably heard someone say, "This isn't authentic to me," when they're presented with things like a new selling script, or proactively asking for the close on the first interaction. This is, without a doubt, the most consistent pushback I hear in response to just about any tactical training, not just that we provide but across industries, disciplines, and backgrounds.

The most critical problem with this line of thinking is that we've lost the meaning of the word authentic.

People tend to think of authenticity as "personally true," or "unique to my identity." In reality, the word comes from the Greek roots autos (self) and hentes (doer). Authenticity is not a passive state, it's an active verb, and you don't create your own personal authenticity without striving. The *true* definition of authenticity, is that you only find your "self" through doing, through being actively uncomfortable, through growth. So when you hear the phrase, "my authentic self is my best self," that's still true. It just doesn't mean what society has programmed us to believe it does.

Since the moment you were born, you've changed and evolved as a person an infinite number of times. You've been programmed and instructed. You've adopted beliefs, rejected beliefs, and adopted more beliefs. You're a dramatically different person now than you were 10 years ago, 5 years ago, even 5 months ago. So, does that mean you were inauthentic 10 years ago because you're authentic today? Of course not. Because that's an incorrect reading of what authenticity really means.

Real, genuine authenticity is nothing more than a genuine push to grow, evolve, try, fail, succeed, and keep going. As long as you're actively growing and striving, you're authentic to who you were meant to be. You can't be your true authentic self by sitting on the couch and waiting for that next sale to come to you. You have to get out there and get uncomfortable. True, real authenticity can only be achieved by learning, growing, developing, and busting open your comfort zone.

As long as you're striving to become a better version of you, you're leaning into your authentic self. That's true authenticity.

So, let's change your speech pattern around this. Instead of saying, "This feels inauthentic to me" when you're presented with something new, call it like it is. Instead, tell yourself, "This feels uncomfortable to me." True sales warriors are continually looking for a chance to add more strategies, more learnings, and more new ideas, to give themselves an edge over their competitors. That's true authenticity. And that means being comfortable with being uncomfortable.

How do I know this is true? Because I know that the brain is a literal learning machine. It's important not to deprive your brain of what it was created to do. The neural pathways in your brain physically strengthen when you use them, and they shrink when you don't. The muscular element of your brain constantly wants to be worked out. When you say, "I won't do this new selling strategy because I've been doing it my own authentic way for 20 years," your positive intention is to be yourself. In reality, you're choosing comfort over authenticity, and that isn't being yourself. It's denying yourself. It's rejecting the opportunity to exceed your current standard. Stepping away from your comfort zone is a risk that takes guts, no question, but the rewards are so much greater than you can imagine at that moment.

In Amy Cuddy's groundbreaking TED Talk, "Your Body Language May Shape Who You Are," she found something huge: you can physically "fake" it until you become it. Want to be more confident socially? Position your body a certain way for long enough, and you'll eventually feel like social Superman. In your next sales call, hold your hands up in victory for two minutes. It may seem strange at first, but it scientifically works. Your testosterone levels shoot up by 8-10%, and your cortisol levels drop at the same rate, meaning your body is physically making you more prepared for action.

Is this any less authentic than you are right now? Of course not, it's actually more authentic. Remember the root? Self + doer = authenticity. By embodying the strategies proven to bring you success, you're living into your mission as an authentic person. You're growing.

The main reason sales training doesn't stick is because salespeople don't believe the strategies they've learned are authentic to them. But now you know that nothing could be more authentic than finding the tension between complacency and mastery, living inside that tension, and using it to grow your skills, ability, and inner strength.

Nothing could be more critical to the true sales warrior than that.

APPLICATION

Progress equals happiness, but as you now know, it also equals authenticity. Which means that the more you focus on making progress every day, the more authentic to your own self you'll personally become.

Use this mental rehearsal technique to ensure that, no matter the circumstance, you're chasing authenticity and growing closer to your authentic being. The one that you were intended to be.

1. Come up with a selling scenario that you want to improve upon this week. For example, it could be handling objections, or asking for the close.

2. Take a 3x5 note card and write out the steps you need to achieve your goal. Then write what success looks like for you once you achieve the improvement you want. What do you see, feel, and hear the moment you achieve it? Make sure you have that image in your mind as vividly as possible. See it through your eyes, hear it through your ears, be cognizant of what you smell.

3. Mentally practice what you need to do to achieve your goal, be sure to include how you will see, feel, hear when you achieve it. Complete this exercise every day for the following 5 days as you strive toward your goal.

4. Filter your daily decisions through that model and ask yourself, "Is this moving me closer to, or away from, becoming my authentic self?"

14

YOUR SUPPORT SYSTEMS DEFINE YOU

"I consciously surround myself with people who actively support my goals."

There's an ancient Buddhist story about a group of different sized rocks placed into a single bag. Hypothetically speaking, you place your bag of rocks in your pocket and spend the next 100 years walking around with them. When you finally take the rocks out of the bag, they're no longer the same rocks you put in your pocket 100 years ago. Their varying angles and textures have all smoothed into the same size and shape because they've rubbed against each other and smoothed out over time.

The rocks all conformed to the others around them. You didn't chip away at them with your own hands. Just by being in proximity to one another they became exactly the same.

The same thing happens to people in relationships. I remember when I was a teenager, I spent my time with a group of guys all wanting to be cool. When they all decided to have that side-spiked haircut, I found myself slathering my hair with gel in the mirror. When my best friends were wearing Z. Cavaricci pants, I found myself swaggering down the hallway in a pair of my own. I try not to dwell on those truly dark times, but it's a great reminder that we pick up what the people we're close to put down.

Maybe you're now thinking about past friendships, or relationships, where you woke up one morning and realized, "this isn't who I am," or in my case, "what the heck is going on with my hair?" Maybe your once-angelic son or daughter started hanging out with the wrong crowd and started cutting class and talking back to you. The fact is, that when you spend so much time surrounded by people, good or bad, you start to morph into them.

Right now, you're conforming yourself to the people you spend the most time with. The key is to be aware of the effect that's having on your sales success. In the end, you'll either sink to their level, stay on their level and never improve, or rise to their level and become better than you were yesterday. You always want to choose peers who drive you to be better than you were yesterday.

This is also important as far as the people you allow to give you feedback. Teddy Roosevelt has a brilliant quote about the benefit of the arena, which encompasses what you do every day.

> **"It is not the critic who counts; not the man
> who points out how the strong man stumbles,
> or where the doer of deeds could have done
> them better. The credit belongs to the man
> who is actually in the arena, whose face is
> marred by dust and sweat and blood."**

What he's saying is that the only feedback that matters comes from people who've done what you do. It doesn't come from the critics on the outside. That's why you need to limit the number of people you allow to give you feedback.

Behavioral researcher, Brené Brown, established this quick and easy process for qualifying your arena.

1. They should only be people who've done what you've done before.
2. Your list should be able to fit on a one-inch by one-inch piece of paper.
3. They should be people who know you and have your best interests at heart.

Feedback is the path to mastery, but the wrong feedback from the wrong people will sink you.

As you take an honest look at the people in your life, this should be a liberating exercise, not an anxiety-driven one. This isn't a call to leave behind any family, friends, or peers who aren't in your arena, or who don't have the same ambitions or goals as you. But it does mean that if you feel actively held back by anyone close to you, it's time to have a tough conversation.

I call this the "here's what it's going to take" conversation. You may be asking when this is necessary, so let me give you an example. A friend of mine named Ashley, told me a story about her husband who interviewed for a sales management position at a car dealership. She told me they interviewed her as well because they wanted to make sure that he was being supported at home. They knew, given the long hours and extra effort, a strong support system was imperative to his success.

If the expectations and behaviors around your goals aren't clear, then tension with your peers and loved ones is inevitable.

The key isn't to just assume your peers are in line with your goals. It's to explain to that group of friends that maybe you won't be able to make as many happy hours, but it doesn't mean you value them any less. Or explain to your significant other that you might be late for dinner some nights, but you're working to build a better future for the entire family down the road. That buy-in is everything, and it must be done up front.

A sales warrior is bombarded by so many adverse situations with prospects on a daily basis that they can't afford to take friendly fire from the rear. I lean on my peers in the Entrepreneur's Organization for support because they're in the arena. They understand my struggles, and they have my best interests at heart. As a result, I'm continually strengthened. That's why your support system is a crucial part of the foundation for a warrior mindset.

APPLICATION

The most essential part of creating a support system that pushes your achievement to new levels, is to take the first step. This means consciously gravitating toward people who build into your goals and contribute to your future success.

Here's your guide to creating a support system that can help you achieve the goals you've set for yourself.

1. Identify the people who aren't adding support, inspiration, and love into your life. Commit to having a conversation with those people to get on the same page so they can be a part of your support system.

2. Identify the people currently in your support system, and write out the characteristics that they have that propel you forward. Write out some additional characteristics you'd like in your support system as well.

3. Use that list of characteristics to look for in the members of your support group. Make sure they align with what you want to accomplish.

4. Recruit people with those characteristics to join your group. Tell them what you appreciate about them, what you'd like the group to accomplish mutually, and what specifically about them you cherish and admire.

5. Commit to the duration and frequency of your meetings on a monthly basis. Make sure it's sustainable, and repeatable, for everyone in the group.

6. Collaborate on the constitution and goals of the group. Make sure everyone has buy-in around the group's collective and individual goals.

15

LIVE BY YOUR PRIMARY QUESTION

"My focus is fixed on moving sales forward every day."

When you wake up every morning, what's the first thought that pops into your mind? I'm guessing that you mentally run through your to-do list each morning as you brush your teeth and get ready for your day. I used to do the same thing. I'd sit at my kitchen table with my coffee and go through a mental checklist of all the tasks I had to accomplish that day, and it was an incredibly helpful way to plan my days.

But it's not the warrior way.

I found that when I focused my day on multiple tasks, or one or two bigger tasks, I became overwhelmed, and caught up in the details, which killed my productivity. I'd quickly get overwhelmed and behind the eight ball.

Every human being wakes up every day with a primary question. You might wake up on Monday, and your primary question is to work through a leads list. On Tuesday, it might be to deliver a presentation. But instead of making those specific tasks your primary question, your primary question should stay the same every day. Your question should be the fuel for your job tasks, rather than the tasks themselves. So, what do I mean by that?

Every sales warrior has the same primary question: **How can I move a sale forward today?**

Just the same, every sales coach has their same primary question: **How can I coach a sale forward today?** That's the driving force behind everything a sales warrior does on a daily basis. It's not about breaking the company sales record every day, or setting some massive personal milestone every day, it's about the process. It's about moving a sale one step closer to the close every single day. It's about making that next call, or handling that next objection, or creating that next raving fan.

One of my favorite stories I've ever heard is about Jim McCann, the founder of 1-800-Flowers. In order to keep the office focused, he posted signs all around his company that said three simple words: **Sell More Flowers.**

While he observed people working, he would randomly ask them, "is this helping you to sell more flowers?" If not, he would redirect their behavior to something that did. He empowered employees to coach up, by asking their bosses, "but will this help us sell more flowers?" It was by this primary question that McCann built 1-800-Flowers into a billion-dollar company.

Your primary question isn't about your specific tasks, it's about your purpose. Think of it like the filter that those daily tasks run through. When the things you do every day filter through your primary question, they should either fall through because they're beneficial, or they should be filtered out and delegated. The key is that your primary question is filtering through things that help you move a sale forward, and filtering out things that don't.

At FPG, every employee on the team has posters with their primary question hanging at their desk. "How can I move a sale forward today?" "How can I increase the speed and profitability of FPG?" "How can I strengthen FPG's content today?" My team has an unbreakable focus on their primary question, and at the end of each day they get to go home feeling accomplished about today's work, instead of anxious about tomorrow's. It's the same for my primary question, which is, "How can I be leading edge today?"

You need to be aware of your primary question at all times. When you prioritize tasks based on your primary question, you'll be more productive, you'll be happier, and you may find that you contribute more to the growth of your company every single day.

One of the immediate after effects of the primary question is that it dramatically improves your goal level. The way Behavioral Sciences Research Press (BSRP) defines goal level as the process of creating a reliable connection between your motivation level, the physical energy you have to accomplish your goals, and your goal itself, what you get out of it. It's like the wire connecting the wall outlet (your motivation) to the TV (your goal).

BSRP says that there are three main aspects to connecting your motivation to what you actually want to achieve. The following definitions are my interpretations of what they are assessing.

1. **The target.** The level of clarity of your goal.
2. **The strategy.** The specific plan to achieve your goal.
3. **The pursuit.** How much energy you're putting towards your strategy.

The entire purpose of your primary question, is that it programs your mind to lock onto your target with your Reticular Activating System (something we'll discuss more with our Lock On strategy), gives you a strategy to achieve it, and pushes you to follow through on the pursuit.

In other words, your primary question is your vital goal achievement companion.

One of the greatest benefits of the primary question, is the human need of certainty. Think about the most stressful parts of your day. What do they all have in common? Uncertainty. If you can't prioritize your tasks based on that primary question, then you're like the person who builds their house on sand instead of stone. Once a big enough wave comes along – a request from another department, an unexpected project, a tough conversation with a boss – then that house topples over.

The primary question is the stone foundation for the day. It mentally centers you as a sales warrior on exactly what you need to do that day. If you're pulled away from moving sales forward, then you know exactly how to find your way back. This is the mentality that separates a sales warrior, who moves sales forward, from everyone else.

APPLICATION

Your primary question is only valuable if it's used intentionally and consistently. This requires a total way of thinking. You need to commit to seeing every one of your tasks through the lens of your primary question.

When you follow these steps to prioritize your primary question above all else, you'll find your results increase and your anxiety decrease.

1. Write out your primary question. For a sales warrior, "How can I move a sale forward today?"; For a sales coach, "How can I coach a sale forward today?" Put it somewhere on your desk where you'll see it every day.

2. Commit to starting your week using your primary question to come up with your weekly goals. Remember, filter every one of your tasks through your primary question. If you're pulled off course by something outside your primary question, use it to get back on track quickly.

3. Commit to ending each week by affirming yourself, and validating someone on your team for accomplishing a goal using their primary question. For example, at FPG, everyone ends each week with our "I'm Freakin' Awesome" Friday Happy Hour with the following statement: **"I'm freakin' awesome in pursuit of my primary question of how can I move a sale forward today, because (something I did that week in alignment with my primary question). That caused (what happened), and the effect of that will be (insert here)."**

16

THE GIFT OF RITUALS

> "My rituals form my success."

I want you to think of your success like a bank account. You don't fill up your bank account accidentally. You make continual deposits you earned through hard work. What happens when you ignore your bank account? It depletes. That's when you start to feel anxious, uncertain, and everything begins to unravel at the seams.

Think of your bank deposits as your rituals, and each deposit is adding to your success. If you don't make those ritual deposits into your bank, you're rapidly draining your mental account until it gets down to nothing. If your deposits are irregular, a big payday one month with nothing the next, you'll heap unnecessary amounts of stress into your life as you try to find out how to pay the bills.

Your rituals actually rewire your brain to focus on achieving a desired goal. A ritual is a way to refocus your attention on your goal, and then reinforce every action to align with your goals.

This, above everything else, is why your rituals shape your life.

Goal-seeking inevitably results in stress, and rituals are a way for sales warriors to clean out all the mental leashes holding you in check. If your goal is to make your company's top performers club, then incorporating a morning ritual around visualizing that reality is a great way to bring that goal to life.

It's just a fact of life that uncertainty brings out a stress response from your brain. I'm sure you can remember times in your life when you had a huge goal, but became too overwhelmed to see it through. This is because your brain was more focused on the outside noise than the goal itself. When we give more power to the circumstances around our goals, than our goals themselves, we burn out and give up.

In Brazil, researchers studied people who perform something called "sim-patias." These are rituals the locals used for achieving goals, like quitting smoking, and curing asthma. Whenever they faced a hardship, the locals would do things like burn leaves, put leaves in a bag, put the bag on a cross-roads, and repeat it for seven days. What they found was game-changing. The study revealed that the people who used these rituals were able to successfully reach their goals when they consciously performed them for a goal-setting purpose.

So even if burning leaves didn't physically change anything, it did in the minds of the people who undertook the ritual. They used the repetition to reframe their mindset for the better, no matter how trivial the action was. It wasn't about the actual activities themselves, it was the importance of the broader ritual and what those people wanted to see, hear, and feel. They didn't just have a ritual, like a lucky dollar, and hope for the best. They used their ritual to refocus their energy on a mental goal, and it worked.

In other words, rituals rewire your brain for the better.

Just the same, my rituals form the basis of my day, and they're always pointing me toward goal achievement. Every morning and evening, I have a carefully laid out multi-step process that allows me to start every day with maximum energy and gratitude, and end each day with the techniques that give me the best chance for success the next day.

Your day either owns you, or you own your day. I couldn't own my day without my rituals. Here's what my mornings look like from Monday-Friday.

> **4:30 a.m.**
> **What I do:** Wake up, meditate, journal.
> **Why I do it:** I need to center myself at the start of every day. Clearing my mind allows me to visualize the success I want to have.
>
> **6:00 a.m.**
> **What I do:** Plan the day, look at my calendar, listen to my customized Amazon 15-minute flash news briefing, use my Halo Neurostimulator, listen to a podcast or audiobook, and have my morning shake.
> **Why I do it:** I'm constantly looking for the minimum effective dose to get me going. This 45-minute period gives me the energy to get started.
>
> **6:45 a.m.**
> **What I do:** High intensity 45-minute workout.
> **Why I do it:** Health is everything. My morning workout is an energizer, allowing me to walk into my office with confidence.
>
> **8:00 a.m.**
> **What I do:** Second breakfast: protein drink, eggs, bacon, cheese, avocado, and beans.
> **Why I do it:** Adding protein to support my workout rounds out my pre-work routine.

8:15 a.m.

What I do: Morning huddle with my team.

Why I do it: My company runs on daily 15-minute stand-up huddles. It gives us clarity, purpose, and motivation to charge into every day.

8:30 a.m.

What I do: Initiate contact with at least one new or existing prospect.

Why I do it: Getting myself in the sales flow with an actual prospect, as quickly as possible, programs me to sell fast.

The bigger question you may be asking yourself is, do rituals like these actually improve performance? In a word: yes. Think about different cultures around the world. Culture is manifested in each society, and it shows in the external world through ritual. People use narratives and artistic production to encode people to live by their culture's beliefs.

In other words, every ritual has a purpose. Find yours and create more space for your conscious mind to do the incredible.

APPLICATION

If you need a place to start, here are four steps to create your own rituals.

1. Form the awareness that you already have around your morning and evening rituals. Identify the ones that benefit you and the ones that don't. Write out the morning and evening rituals you currently have.

2. Have compassion around the fact that your rituals are giving you what you are currently getting. Finish the following sentence: "I am grateful that my rituals have allowed me to accomplish _____"

3. Ask yourself these two questions:

   a. "What new outcomes do I want out of each and every day?"

   b. "How do I want to feel at the end of my morning and evening rituals?"

4. Hack your morning and evening rituals to achieve your desired outcomes by creating new behaviors.

Your rituals could include anything from journaling, to meditation, to exercise. Be conscious about the last thoughts you have before you go to bed. Meditate, or listen to music, to put yourself in an optimal state. When you consciously form your rituals around the goals you set and the outcomes you want, you're taking another tangible step toward becoming the sales warrior.

17

BE YOUR OWN SUPPORT, INSPIRATION, AND LOVE

> " I am my own source of support, inspiration, and love. "

You already know that your results come from your root programming, but what happens in between? How does your programming convert into what you're currently getting from a results perspective?

That's what the Consciousness Chart, and more specifically the Results Matrix, will tell you.

THE CONSCIOUSNESS CHART

I **AM** ENOUGH!

LOVED	GRATEFUL	LOVE	MASTERY	MENTOR
INSPIRED	ACCOUNTABLE	PURPOSEFUL	CHALLENGE	COLLABORATE
SUPPORTED	HOPEFUL	TRUST	IMPROVEMENT	ENGAGE

RESULTS MATRIX

PROGRAMMING	BELIEFS	EMOTIONS	MOTIVATION	BEHAVIOR
DENIED	ANGER	HATE	COMPETE	CHEAT
CONDEMNED	HOPELESS	BLAME	CRUISE	SABOTAGE
DESPISED	SHAME	HUMILIATION	NOT LOSE	ESCAPE

I **AM NOT** ENOUGH!

The Results Matrix is the line between programming and results. All of us are programmed by our past, by our experiences, by our parents, by our culture, and by our peers. This programming leads you to have certain beliefs about the world. Those beliefs influence your emotions, which influence your motivations. Those motivations influence your everyday behaviors, and those behaviors are what lead to your results. It's all connected, and the root of the tree is the way you've been programmed by the past, and the way you're currently programming yourself.

On a broader level, there are positive and negative feelings that emerge from each level on The Results Matrix. If you're negatively programmed, for instance, you feel denied, condemned and despised. You feel denied in the sense that you feel like no one's listening to you. You feel condemned in the sense that you can't control your fate. And you feel despised in the sense that you've been rejected.

It's not below the line to feel this way, we've all been there at one point in our lives, but it is below the line to linger there.

I've heard every justification for why people stay in these mental spaces, but the most common is to deflect the blame outward. They'll say "The reason I'm not above the line is because I don't have any support, inspiration, or love in my life." When you go above the line, those are the three prevailing feelings: you feel supported, inspired, and loved. Any programming that gives you those three root feelings is positive, and will ultimately lead you to the results you crave.

So again, why would anyone justify their own denied, condemned or despised feelings? It's because they have a leaky bucket.

Let's back up for a minute and think about what happens when you get any kind of support, inspiration, and love from others. Salespeople with positive programming can survive on one piece of positive feedback for weeks. You can tell them, "Great job on your prospecting calls yesterday, I'm proud of all the appointments you set," and they'll be motivated to keep going. But give that same feedback to people with negative programming? It'll fall right through their mental bucket, and they'll be back needing more positive feedback in another 24 hours.

The person who needs validation every 24 hours isn't really seeking support, validation, and love. They're seeking approval. And approval doesn't last.

Imagine that the events in your life are like a bucket full of water, and everything in your life that isn't serving your purpose is like a hole in your bucket. The only way you can patch up those holes is by looking inward at your own mindset. You can't control your external circumstances. If you have leaders who don't give you that positive programming, then you have to embody that within yourself. So if you have a leader who tells you, "If you come to me and don't know how to sell something, it means I hired the wrong person for the job." Then you need to have the resources to be your own support, inspiration, and love.

Take Larry Ellison. Ellison was programmed from the time he was born to believe he wasn't enough. He was born in the Bronx to a single mother, and when he caught pneumonia at nine months old, she sent him to Chicago to be raised by her aunt and uncle.

As Ellison grew up, his adoptive father repeatedly told him he was "good for nothing." But Ellison didn't allow those words to penetrate his mindset. He drowned out those negative voices and used them as fuel to prove them wrong. This man, who was programmed to believe that he would never amount to anything, founded The Oracle Corporation years later. In 2018, Ellison's net worth was estimated at $58 billion, making him the 10th richest person in the world. Despite his surroundings, despite his programming, and despite his rough upbringing, he became his own source of support, inspiration, and love, and became something great.

As children, we're constantly being programmed. It's just a fact of life. A tangible step in the maturation process is recognizing that as we get older, we have the power to take control of our programming for ourselves.

It all stems from gratitude. If your programming is below the line, you're always worried, you see threats around every corner, and you need approval with every action. There's no gratitude in that. If your programming is above the line, then every result, whether positive or negative, comes from a root of gratitude. Lose a sale? You're grateful for what you learned. Move a sale forward? You're grateful for the coaching that helped you get to that point.

Either way, you are your own source of support, inspiration, and love. And that's how you program yourself for the results you want.

APPLICATION

When you can successfully disassociate from things that keep you from becoming your own support, inspiration, and love, and fully recognize that they do not define you, you'll have greater freedom and more control over your life. Follow these steps to have courage around pushing aside your leashes, and become your own support, inspiration, and love.

1. Acknowledge any past programming that gives you a negative feeling. Then replace it with something more beneficial via positive programming sources like TED Talks, audiobooks, or life-affirming podcasts.

2. Make a habit of looking into the mirror every morning and telling yourself out loud, "I choose to let go of any leashes that are holding me back. I know that my true authentic self is my courageous self that releases my leashes."

3. Ask yourself each day, "What actions or attitudes show that I have a leash?" Write those down.

4. Ask, "What action can I take to move towards _____ and move away from _____."

5. Decide to take action and measure your results.

18

SETBACKS ARE JUST COMEBACKS IN DISGUISE

" I cannot fail, I can only learn and grow. "

How we handle our setbacks is far more important than how we handle success. We all experience setbacks in life, and our attitude about those setbacks is what determines whether we bounce back or fall hard.

The first time I lost a client, I thought the world was crashing down around me. It wasn't just the revenue loss. It was what that meant for my company, for me, for our relevance – everything. But as I look at that moment in hindsight, I realize that by having that experience, I was able to refocus my energy and figure out a better way forward. It actually made our company better, because we were able to course correct, adjust, and improve. That's all a setback really is – a small tug telling you it's time to shift gears.

There's no profession on Earth where a person will experience setbacks more on a daily basis than in sales. A salesperson might get rejected by 50 out of 50 prospects on Monday, and they've got to start it all over again with a fresh mindset on Tuesday. It's impossible to overstate how much mental fortitude it takes, not just to overcome those setbacks, but to turn them into something positive.

Sales warriors don't just know how to handle the word "no." They're strengthened by it.

Nobody I know does this better than Jeffrey Hayzlett, a wildly successful entrepreneur, CEO of The C-Suite Network among others, author, and speaker. Early in his career, Hayzlett wrapped up a sales call that didn't go particularly well. As Hayzlett explained his call to a friend, his friend couldn't figure out why he was so upbeat and excited as he talked about this call that ended in an emphatic "no."

"It takes 10 no's to get to a yes," Hayzlett replied. "And that was my 10th one."

That's the mindset of a sales warrior.

I once coached a sales warrior named Michelle, who would bounce back from bad sales experiences with amusement. Laughing, she would say things like, "Well, I really botched that one."

The difference between Michelle, and so many others I've observed, is that she never stayed in that place. She used that experience as a learning tool because she saw the whole thing differently. She was lighthearted about it. Nothing was personal, and so nothing was a failure. That word wasn't even in her mental vocabulary. It was just a learning experience for next time. Michelle used that mentality to rise to become the head of sales at a billion-dollar company.

So often we only focus on the deficit gap in the wake of a negative experience, and not on the abundance gap. Psychologically, the deficit gap is how much below the norm we believe we are as a result of some negative outcome. If someone hangs up the phone in the middle of a sales call, the tendency is to judge yourself based on how poorly the call went versus how much better you wish it would've gone. We dwell on the failure instead of reflecting on the possibility of what we could learn from the experience.

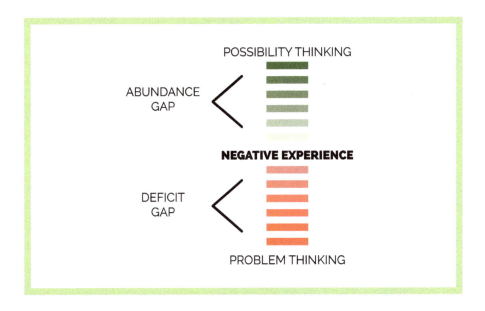

But too often, we don't slow down and look at the abundance gap instead. This mindset flips the script. It looks at how much you've learned as a result of that call, and how much better you'll be, compared with how the call actually went.

So instead of rehashing everything you did wrong in generalities – "I can't believe how poorly that went" – you use the experience by extracting specifics – "Next time I can move the sale forward by getting a position of strength earlier."

"IF YOU LEARNED FROM YOUR MISTAKE, THEN IT WASN'T A MISTAKE."

Now one of Hollywood's most respected directors, Steven Spielberg was rejected by his school of choice, the University of Southern California, for film three different times. But he didn't let that stop him. Spielberg eventually secured an internship at Universal Studios after enrolling in a different college. During that internship, he was asked to direct a small film, with his work impressing Universal executives so much that they offered him a seven-year contract. He became the youngest director ever hired by the studio, and now has an IMDB profile several miles long.

The cherry on top of this story is that he was awarded an honorary degree from USC in 1994, and became trustee of the university in 1996. He joked, "Since 1980, I've been trying to be associated with this school, I eventually had to buy my way in." As of this date, Spielberg has directed 51 films and won three Oscars, and Forbes Magazine puts Spielberg's wealth at $3 billion.

Spielberg could've changed his path after the first rejection from that school, and most of us probably would have by the second rejection, and completely given up by the third. But Spielberg's motivation outweighed his setbacks, and he found his breakthrough.

The military recently completed a study around the after-action reviews they give to soldiers to debrief after combat. When soldiers who failed their missions received reviews over what went wrong, they were more likely to succeed the next time compared to soldiers who received reviews after successful missions. Think about that. The soldiers who failed learned more, and succeeded at a higher rate than the soldiers who were successful.

Just the same, you can turn every single loss into a teachable, learning moment that leads to more wins down the road.

Sales warriors are constantly growing and adapting with every setback. They don't see deficit gaps, only abundance gaps. Everything in your life, including and especially your setbacks, is happening for you, not to you. Finding the teachable lesson in that will gift you with your greatest renewable energy source.

APPLICATION

All you have to do to create buy-in around your ability to stage a comeback is to have awareness around the times you've already done it in the past.

Right now you're going to create your "comeback lifeline." This is going to lay out your history of accomplishment to give you the gratitude for the courage you'll need to push through your future setbacks. And remember, you cannot fail, you can only learn and grow.

1. Write down 10 times in your life when you faced a setback, and how you achieved a comeback.

2. For each instance, write out what you learned, and the specific strategies you used to achieve your comeback.

3. Then write down what each instance did for you, instead of to you.

4. Keep this list close when you hit your next setback. Use the strategies and mental state you had in those previous moments to fuel your current one.

19

YOUR HEALTH IS YOUR WEALTH

" By controlling my physical state, I control my fate. "

Beethoven took long walks every day between creation sessions to refresh his mind. Anna Wintour, the editor-in-chief for *Vogue* magazine, plays a vigorous tennis match for one hour every single day before heading into work. Gwyneth Paltrow, not only gets up at 4:30 a.m. to practice yoga every morning, but she's a huge advocate for clean eating. Each of these people experienced incredible accomplishments, and their healthy habits are a huge contributing factor.

Sure, each of these success stories have many other moving parts involved, but there's no denying the link between being healthy and being successful. A University of Georgia study showed that people who exercise regularly are more confident, better able to focus, and more likely to follow through on promises and goals. Researchers also asked 1,300 people, who earn upwards of $100,000 annually, what helped them stay focused, and 75% said physical fitness was a huge part of their drive to keep going.

Your health is the backbone of embodying the mindset of a sales warrior. Good health increases your motivation levels, which helps you move toward your goals, and break your leashes. Without a healthy physical state, your mind rapidly breaks down. It's also the most neglected strategy you'll find in this book because too many people see health as only a physical concern. And it's true that your health controls physical matters like your weight, blood pressure, and cholesterol.

But it has a far more striking impact on your mental state than you probably realize.

Dr. Bruce Lipton is one of the foremost biologists in the world. In his decades of research, he found that less than 10% of all known diseases are due to our genetic coding. There are only six of them. In other words, our health is overwhelmingly being controlled by how we think and how we're programmed on a subconscious level. Even though we don't realize it, we're constantly manifesting illness into our lives by thoughts that lowers our immune system, change our brain chemistry, and negatively effect our ability to fight off disease.

Neuroscience has recognized that the subconscious mind controls 95% of our lives; it controls how we react, how we think, and how we make decisions. Dr. Lipton's research followed that truth to its logical conclusion: your subconscious mind is controlling your health, too. Which means you have the power to overcome almost any health situation you confront. All it takes is a commitment to change your programming.

Your cognitive health refers to your capacity to think, recall, and process information. Becoming a sales warrior means nurturing your brain, and one of the best ways to nurture your brain is through your bodily health.

Your brain is the organ responsible for every decision you make, every emotion you feel, every word you speak, and every thought you have. That's no surprise of course. But if that's the case, then why do so many people neglect their health and then wonder why their energy levels drop at 2 p.m., or why they struggle to retain focus? That's all health-related, and it's fixable right now.

In 2015, researchers in Finland conducted a fascinating study on twins. The study, authored by professors Jaako Kaprio, Lea Pulkkinen, and Richard Rose, highlighted the role that physical activity plays in health and brain structure. One twin was more physically active than the other twin, and the research found that the more active twin had grown more grey matter in her brain throughout her life.

So why is this a big deal? Grey matter in the brain is mainly responsible for muscle control and sensory perception, so it makes sense that someone who lives a healthy lifestyle would have more of it. But the fascinating thing is that grey matter also plays an enormous role in things like speech, decision making, and self-control, three vital qualities of becoming a sales warrior.

Two genetically identical people, but the physically healthier twin actually changed her brain through a healthy lifestyle. Surprising? Hardly.

You have this power. Exercise releases endorphins, which give you a kind of "high" after your workout. You've probably heard about how these endorphins make you happier, or more energized, but they also increase your work performance as well. These neurotransmitters pass along signals from one neuron to the next, and the functions of these neurons are endless.

Those neurons are specialized cells that transmit impulses throughout your body, and they are the reasons your brain functions at the level it currently does. So by influencing those neurons through healthy habits, you're directly influencing your results.

Here are the eight health essentials that I choose to live by.

1. Regular bloodwork. The content of your blood tells you everything you need to know about things like B12, iron levels, and testosterone. My vitamins are prescribed based on what my blood needs.

2. The Tim Ferriss low-carb diet. I eat five days of low sugar, no white carbs, high fat, and high protein. Then I can eat what I want during the weekend.

3. I have a morning shake that consists of:
   1. Protein powder
   2. Liquid egg whites
   3. Bulletproof Brain Octane Oil
   4. Keto Fuel
   5. Energy Pre-workout powder
   6. Lemon juice
   7. Apple cider vinegar

4. I monitor my alkaline and acidic levels. Cancer can't survive in an alkaline state.

5. Lots of green juice (I recommend Athletic Greens).

6. Yerba Mate tea for a no-spike energy drink. Yerba Mate is a traditional South American brew that's been said to offer the "strength of coffee, the health benefits of tea, and the euphoria of chocolate" all in one beverage.

7. Three 45-minute high-intensity workouts each week with a personal trainer to create accountability.

8. Listen to The Model Health Show podcast on how to maximize my mind and body.

These eight steps keep me from getting sick while owning three companies and traveling every week. They fuel me to finish athletic events like a 13-mile a Spartan Race. But I'm not an exception. You can do the same thing, all it takes is commitment.

APPLICATION

You don't just wake up one morning and completely change your routine to live a healthy life. That's why so many new year's resolution diets and exercise plans fail. Living your healthiest life is a gradual process, and I would never expect anyone to completely change their habits overnight. So, here's how you can start living a healthier life without facing burnout.

1. Assess your current state.
   - Write out any areas that you want to improve. This could include any sleeping, exercise, or eating habits that you'd like to see improve.

2. Find your why.
   - Next to your assessments, write out why and how changing that aspect will improve your life. Every goal needs a why to fuel it. Circle it back to your primary question. How will this change help you achieve that goal?

3. Get your goals together
   - Write down where you want to be with each health goal, and by when. Make a realistic plan of action so you can become at least 1% better every single day. You don't have to make extreme changes overnight, just aim for that one step forward, no matter how small or large.

4. Commit.
   - Setting the goals is the easy part, sticking to those goals is where everything can fall apart. Commit to improving by that 1% every day by finding a close friend or partner to hold you accountable. Maybe you and your partner will start cooking healthier together. Maybe you can find a workout partner to run with you before work each morning. Don't be afraid to reach out for help, it's much easier to accomplish a goal when you're not in it alone.

Here's an example of what one of my health-goal plans looks like:

I want to exercise every morning **because it will** fuel my brain and body with the energy I need **to** move a sale forward today. **I commit to** three 45-minute high-intensity workouts each week **with** a personal trainer **to create accountability.**

20

INSPIRATION THROUGH MOTIVATION

"I have all the physical and mental energy I need to achieve my goals."

True motivation originates from two sources: physiology and psychology. When both of those streams come together, they create one gigantic rushing river: the motivation of a sales warrior.

Motivation isn't about what a person says they believe – motivation is a fruit-based activity. It's about what people actually see as a result of your actions. Truly motivated sales warriors are more energized, more engaged, more driven, and produce greater results. And here's the good news: people who are displaying motivated behaviors aren't genetically different from people who aren't. They've just chosen a series of life patterns that created a motivated mindset, and that drove them to do exceptional things.

Above all else, sales warriors are driven by consistency, and true motivation creates consistency.

Motivation is the amount of energy you have to move toward your goals. The way BSRP describes motivation is energy; it's having sufficient energy to accomplish your goals and, in my words, remove any leashes you have that keep you from acting.

On a root level, motivation is the internal force that drives you to do something. For instance, if you're not prospecting because you feel like you don't want to, it's a motivation issue. Physically, you could have low motivation because of habits like excessive smoking, improper diet, or lack of exercise. Mentally, motivation dips are usually the cause of stories we tell ourselves all the time: "I'm not capable of doing this", "My boss doesn't care about me", or, "This isn't what I want to do". Thoughts like these are like mental weight gain; they do nothing but slow you down.

Salespeople are constantly being externally motivated: by their boss ("I need you to get this done"), by their circumstances (Friday's deadline) or by their peers ("I need your help with this"). Everyone has external motivations. Not everyone has internal motivations, but sales warriors do.

Purely externally motivated salespeople are continually limiting themselves because they're motivated by things out of their locus of control. If money is your motivation, what happens when you lose a sale? If your motivation is power, what happens when you're passed up for a promotion? When your primary source of motivation comes from external sources, and those don't materialize, that entire construct of motivation falls apart. You're left with nothing.

Self-motivation, on the other hand, is the motivation to achieve that comes from a sincere desire to be better for your own sake. This is the motivation to become a stronger speaker in front of groups to create your own self-confidence. Or the motivation to prospect, because you want to beat your own record for sales won in a day.

Becoming self-motivated is a total mindset shift from outside to inside. When you're externally motivated, you're made of glass. You're driven by the results of your work and when you don't receive them, you shatter. When you're self-motivated, you have an unbreakable spine of steel. You're driven by your own desire to improve, and as a result, you're unbreakable. When outside circumstances no longer *drive* you, they can no longer *affect* you.

You can't make yourself want to sell through external motivators, but you can create that want by finding your motivation within yourself.

Scientists have found three primary reasons why people aren't motivated. Due to chemical reactions in your brain, you tell yourself one of three stories. When the resistance to something is really large, you tell yourself more than just one.

1. I have to do this.
2. I don't feel right about doing this.
3. I can't do this.

Again, these are all externally-motivated, weakening thoughts, not internally-motivated, empowering thoughts. They feed off your past setbacks, your own resistance to change, or your belief that life is happening to you. None of these beliefs will benefit you in any circumstance, big or small.

Just think of the opposite.

1. I want to do this.
2. I feel right about doing this.
3. I can do this.

How much more empowering is that? All it takes is a mindset shift. In fact, you can make that shift by the time you finish this strategy.

On our Consciousness Chart, motivation is the Mastery Pyramid. The key is that below the line behavior is always "playing to" something, while an above the line mentality is always "playing for" something. When you're genuinely in a place of learning and growing, it comes from a deep place within. It comes from your own burning desire to become a better version of you, and that's where all true sales warrior motivation comes from.

Your brain can be a vicious editor, which can play havoc on your motivation. In order to get to the bottom of your motivation, you have to get around the negative mental editing your brain does to your goals (You might think, "This is too difficult," or, "I'm not up for this.") and get to the heart of your own personal motivation. Your motivation has to be stronger than the sacrifices you will make to achieve your goals.

APPLICATION

In order to do this, you're going to learn how to dive deep into the emotional motivation locked within your own mind and bring it back up to the surface. Doing this will give you the emotional fuel you need to move forward towards success.

1. Take 15 minutes and write out the truths behind your biggest current goal. Ask yourself:

    - Why does this goal matter to me?
    - How will this goal change my life?
    - What will I need to do to achieve this goal?
    - Who will be affected by this goal?
    - When do I want to achieve this goal?
    - Where will this goal lead me?

2. While you write, don't think or allow your mental editor to come out – just write the first things that come to mind about the emotional motivation behind your goals. This is a technique called "auto-writing," and it will get around any self-editing, and allow you to see the true motivation behind your goals.

3. Call back to this document whenever your motivation behind your goal wanes. Use it to combat your own "I can't do this", "I have to do this", or "I don't feel right about doing this", thoughts. Use this emotional fuel to carry you through and generate your own internal motivation whenever you need it.

21

THE POWER OF YOUR PROCEDURE

" A repeatable process propels me towards success. "

You can separate everyone on the planet into two broad categories: pro-cedurally-based or option-based.

People whose minds are procedural see things as a process to be repeated. Procedure-based brains immediately think "how" when they have a task in front of them. They think *how* they ac-complish something, *how* long they will need, they think of *how* the steps will help them complete a task.

Option-based minds are less ordered. They think *why* this is the way to do something, they think *why* the task needs to be done a certain way, they think *why* one way will work better than another way. Instead of connecting the dots from A to B to C, they might go from C, to A, to B, on Monday, and A, to C, to B, on Tuesday.

Both are equally valid ways of experiencing the world, but only one embodies the mindset of a sales warrior.

And that's the procedurally-based mind.

Everyone uses both to some degree, but the most successful salespeople on earth live and die by their procedures.

Procedurally-based minds thrive on using repeatable processes and laid out steps to accomplish something. Option-based minds try to find the best way for them to accomplish something based on whims, or how they feel in the moment. In short, procedurally-based brains think "how", option-based brains think "why".

"A REPEATABLE PROCESS WILL PROPEL YOU TOWARDS PROFIT."

Think about an airplane pilot. The success of every flight depends on the success of their procedure. The only time they deviate from it is when something unexpected happens, like severe turbulence or, in extreme cases, a blown engine. And in that case, they have separate procedures for those scenarios as well.

In 2017, surgeon, Atul Gawande, researched whether a 19-item checklist would reduce human errors during surgeries. Gawande's team applied this checklist to eight sites in eight cities across the globe. Then they measured the rate of death and complications before and after they started using the checklist.

I'm sure you can guess what happened. The emphasis on procedures caused the mortality rate to drop, and the number of surgical complications diminished. When they had a process in place, they literally saved lives.

Just the same, a sales warrior knows that sales boils down to 80% science and 20% art. The science is the procedures you know to follow to maximize your success. This is someone who thinks in systems and processes, who is open to adopting a new process, and will work extremely procedurally and follow the science so they can let the score take care of itself. I know that procedurally-based sales warriors will outperform option-based salespeople every time.

The place where option-based tendencies emerge most with salespeople, is during conflict. Consider about what people do when they get stressed: they go shopping, or they change up their routine and do something spontaneous or offbeat.

That may work as a coping mechanism, but it doesn't work in sales. There's actually no better time to follow your process than when you get a tricky objection, or when the prospect says "no". It just takes repetition, commitment, and mindfulness to make it happen. At FPG, the beneficial brain science behind the procedurally-based warrior mindset, is why our programs are so tactical. We know it works. And the proof is in our clients' sales success.

If you're naturally option-based, don't panic. I believe anyone can do anything, so becoming more procedurally-based is… a process (surprise). You can consciously shift toward procedures by embracing them, not moving away from them. Spend some time each morning organizing your day. Learn a selling process and commit to using it 100% of the time. Plan out your cold call structure. These are all steps to program yourself to become more procedural.

And every time to do it, you'll notice yourself becoming more and more comfortable adding your own art to your science-based process.

APPLICATION

A repeatable process will propel you towards profit. But first, you need to become aware of the benefits you're moving toward by being procedurally-based, and the negatives you're moving away from.

So, let's start taking those steps towards success.

1. Identify what's valuable to you about becoming more procedurally-based as a sales warrior.
   a. Write it down as, "This is important to me because _____"

2. List out five positive benefits that becoming more procedurally-based as a salesperson will bring you. Think in terms of how you'll become more confident, assured, or successful in relation to thinking in "how" terms.

3. List out five negative outcomes that becoming more procedurally-based will help you move away from. This can be anything from ambiguity, to stress, to missed sales.

4. Keep these lists close to you as a reminder to follow your process. Memorize your lists so you can embody these realities, and become a procedural sales warrior.

22

THERE IS NO TALENT WITHOUT EFFORT

"Talent is nothing more than effort in disguise."

If you believe that the skills you have today are from raw, natural, talent. I'm about to burst your bubble. The harsh truth is that you weren't born with any gifts, and you didn't get where you are today by just existing. You may have been born with *tendencies*, but true talent is *earned*.

Sure, you might have a natural *passion* for something, but that doesn't automatically mean you'll have *talent* for it. Jimi Hendrix was an incredibly talented musician, and an especially talented guitarist. But Hendrix didn't just pick up a guitar and play like a rock star, he used his **natural passion** for the music **to develop his talent**.

"TALENT IS EARNED."

The word "talented" gets thrown around a lot in sales circles. "He's a naturally talented closer", or, "She's a naturally talented networker". It's a convenient way to put mental distance between the achievement of others and where we currently are at the moment. But the pure definition of talent is one of those root definitions that we've gradually lost touch with over the centuries.

Talent actually comes from the medieval Latin root *talenta*, which means "inclination, will, or desire". Talent itself isn't a born trait; it's developed and created through sheer will and desire. And all you need to do to confirm this as the truth, is look at the anatomy of your brain.

Different people might be born with slightly more natural ability in a specific area, but science shows that effort always overcomes genetics. When you see an Olympic athlete breaking the world sprinting record, or a math whizz mentally creating multi-digit calculations, it's easy to assume they're just blessed with skills beyond our own. It's also easy to rationalize their success as nothing more than winners in a genetic lottery. When you do this, you give up your own ability to ever reach that level. You're giving up your own agency. That doesn't mean you'll ever run as fast as Usain Bolt, or go to the moon like Buzz Aldrin, but it also doesn't mean you *won't*.

The truth is that there is scientifically almost no connection between a person's "natural" talent and their capacity for success. Multiple studies bear this truth out. Someone might be born with natural speed, but someone born with zero natural speed will surpass them if they out-train them.

J.P. Piccinini is the CEO of JP and Associates REALTORS, one of the nation's fastest growing multi-billion dollar realtor brokerages. Piccinini started his own business and basically worked out of the trunk of his car for the first year. He'd wake up at 4 a.m. and did everything, from the operations to the paperwork to the selling of homes. In other words, Piccinini put in the work.

He learned how to sell homes. He learned about the business. He wasn't born with that talent. He worked at it. And seven years later, the company hit $2 billion and rising.

You'll hear stories like this from entrepreneurs everywhere. And the one lesson you hear over and over again? That effort trumps talent.

Daniel Coyle's book, *The Talent Code*, proved that effort creates talent, not the other way around. When you stress the wiring in your brain with repetition, it builds up something called myelin in your brain. This is the coating that wraps around your neural pathways. The more you do something, the more myelin you build up around that wire. And the more myelin you build up, the faster the signal moves across those wires, and the better you are at something.

But you aren't born with these strong myelin connections, they don't just grow on their own, you create them.

Like anything else, sales is an industry built on repetition and process. I've seen trainers claim that selling ability is something you're born with, which is a dangerous idea. For one, that releases people from this idea of creating their own talent. The meaning of your communication isn't the intention of your words, it's the response it provokes. Throwing your hands up and saying, "I'm not a born salesperson" is the result of programming that says that talent comes from genetics, not repetition. And, as you now know, that simply isn't true.

Take me, for example. Early in my professional speaking career, someone told me that I would never become a professional speaker. I didn't have the talent, he said. I was too awkward in front of crowds, my delivery wasn't good enough, I didn't have enough natural stage presence. That lit a fire underneath my motivation. What if I could prove him wrong? So I doubled down on training, and I eventually became the youngest ever member of the National Speaker Association's Million Dollar Speaker Group. Pretty good for someone with no talent, right?

Developing your talent in sales is the same as learning to play guitar. Both are full of soaring successes, and difficult setbacks.

When you first start playing guitar, your fingers begin to feel numb as you perfect the basic chords. You finally move on and start forming callouses on your fingertips as you pick up the pace. And just when you think you'll be an Eric Clapton in no time, you get stuck on a tricky chord and become tempted to smash your guitar against your wall. But imagine if Jimi Hendrix threw away his guitar just because he got frustrated during the learning process.

"BECOME THE BEST BY STUDYING THE BEST."

Developing your talent can be a disappointing process. I've been there. But I've found that the talent development process is a lot less disappointing when I study someone who has the level of talent that I desire. A mantra I've carried with me is, "become the best by studying the best." I believe that no matter how great you are at something, there's always someone out there who can do it better. Rather than letting this reality discourage you, use it to your advantage.

Your talent comes from your effort, and your effort comes from your ability to grow through setbacks. Setbacks are no longer soul-crushing, because you know they're valuable learning tools that drive you to succeed at a level you didn't think was possible. The key is repetition, reflection, and resolution.

APPLICATION

Learning about someone who is the best at what they do can provide you with a plan on how you can get there too.

I understand that these next steps may sound a little difficult, but I promise they will change your life. I knew a sales warrior who kept a picture of her role model on a corkboard in her office so she could start each day reminded of who she wanted to become. Every time I've had a new goal, or wanted to learn a new skill, I've used this exercise to do that. I spent years and years studying the top sales professionals, so I could become one myself.

The first step is to identify your specific goal. Do you want to double your sales? Do you want to become better at handling objections? Do you want to increase your ability to sell against the competition?

Next, out of everyone in the world, I want you to think of the person you want to be like

Once you have your goal, and your person, it's time to start putting it to work.

1. **Put the person's name or picture in a place where you can see it every day.** This visualization technique will motivate you every single day to stay on the path that will lead you towards your goal.

2. **Learn the habits of this person.** What is this person's routine? What does this person do every day that makes them the best?

3. **Find their story.** Study their story of how they became who they are today. What setbacks did they face? How did they achieve their goals? What was their process?

4. **Model your path after theirs.** Become the best by studying the best, and once you've made it, surpass them. Once you've surpassed them, do it all over again.

23

OWN YOUR SUCCESS

"I am the problem, and I am also the solution."

Growing up, my dad had a phrase he must've told me a thousand times: "Whether you succeed or you fail, it's all on you." When I was initially rejected from TCU, my college of choice, I had that phrase ringing in my head when I walked into the dean's office and pled my case. And it was the motivation for why I was provisionally accepted by the dean that day and graduated three and a half years later with honors.

Today, I proudly tell my kids the same thing. Nobody controls your success, or your failure, except for you.

This is the core concept of the ownership mindset. For a sales warrior, my definition of total ownership is **the unwavering desire to see your company's goals and mission as your own**. The best way for you to embody that ownership mindset is to own, internalize, and chase the goals and the mission of your company. That's the whole idea of being above the line. You're fitting the needs of your company by realizing that the way to achieve *your* goals is to help your company achieve *its* goals.

"CHANGE THE WAY YOU LOOK AT THINGS SO THE THINGS YOU LOOK AT CHANGE."

The Bushido Code was created by the honor-bound Japanese warrior class that universalized the seven virtues of a life well lived. The greatest honor within the Bushido Code is to serve your house and to give your all for the people within your tribe. You accomplish this by living by those virtues. There's nothing more honorable and noble than fulfilling the needs of the people who rely on you every day.

I believe the same holds true for sales warriors when it comes to an ownership mindset. And there are six behaviors to live out this ownership mindset on a daily basis.

1. **Verbally uses the company's standards to make decisions.** You can't make decisions based on the company standards if you don't know them. So take the time to commit your company's standards to memory, and then actively look to apply them to add speed and profitability right away.

2. **Treats the company's resources as their own**. If it was your company, how would your behavior change right now? Could you close that sale at a higher price? Would you be more aware of how you're spending company time? Would you be more aware of how your teammates are talking about your company? Would you take on more responsibility?

3. **Focuses more on what they can give the company than what they get from it.** Your brain is wired to respond to help by helping back. It's called The Law of Reciprocity. And here's the game-changing part: psychologists found that the *response* is usually greater than the initial action. People tend to give back more than they got in the first place.

4. **Actively uses possibility thinking to create solutions for the company.** Instead of focusing on why something *can't* be done – "there's no way we can hit this sales target this month" – sales warriors focus on why something *can* be done – "let's brainstorm on how we can change up our strategy to hit our sales target this month".

5. **Finds new ways to increase company profit margin.** If you're selling something for a certain price, can you upsell/cross-sell to increase the price just a little bit more? If you're already selling an add-on for $400, could you sell it for $450? Or $500? Do you see areas where your company could use its resources better?

6. **Through their advocacy, inspires others to be advocates.** Advocacy isn't just about believing in your company's standards and goals. The definition of an advocate is someone who recommends and supports something *publicly*.

I find so many salespeople have a leash around this concept because they see it as somehow minimizing themselves. If that's you, it's so important for you to change the way you look at things so the things you look at change. I believe the reality is actually the opposite. Being an owner means becoming more, and contributing more, within your company. It doesn't mean minimizing yourself. It means *maximizing* yourself, your impact, and your sales results.

APPLICATION

Being an owner within your company gives you the chance to have even greater influence. And that means attaining mental ownership for your company. It means going above the line so you can be at that ownership level, where you're creating new processes and verbally using your company standards. It means having more responsibility so you can help your peers climb up to your level.

Being an owner means becoming who you were truly meant to be. Follow these steps to become that owner today.

1. Commit to memorizing your company's standards and making at least one verbal decision based on a standard every week.

2. Write down three ways you can use an ownership mindset to treat your company's resources as your own. Then, commit to following through on those things going forward.

3. Come up with one way you can focus on what you can give to your company. At this time, release any thoughts of what you will get in return.

4. Come up with one way you can personally increase your company's profit margin, and put that into action.

24

WARRIOR CURIOSITY

"The more curious I am, the more successful I become."

Something interesting happens in the brain when you make the conscious decision to be curious: you get smarter.

In 2009, researcher, Dr. Colin F. Camerer, made a game-changing discovery: when people are curious to know the answers to something, they learn at a greater rate once they figure it out. In other words, the mental payoff is much greater if you're actively curious to find out the answer. It's like the satisfaction you get when you place that last piece into the puzzle. You've finally revealed the full picture.

I can't tell you how important this is for sales warriors. Salespeople who lack a childlike curiosity will say things like, "If you need anything, I'll be over here," or, "Let me know if there's anything I can help you with". Where's the curiosity in that? Where's the burning desire to find out what problem the prospect is currently dealing with, so you can fundamentally improve their life or their business?

A study conducted by Dr. Charan Ranganath, a psychologist at the University of California, discovered that the human brain retains more information if we're curious about it. The part of your brain that regulates pleasure and reward lights up when your curiosity is piqued. You know what else lights up? Your hippocampus, which is the part of the brain involved in the creation of memories. The more questions you ask, the smarter you become.

Curiosity helps to chemically change your brain to become more mentally engaged in what you're doing. Albert Einstein once said, "I have no special talents. I am only passionately curious." I don't know about you, but I'm following his lead.

As a sales warrior, your curiosity is everything. It's your pathway to growth, to more engaged customers, to more sales. Curiosity means discovery plus enjoyment. It's the best way to motivate yourself for success.

The key is to go something I call "Three Why's Deep." You need to uncover as many "why's" underneath your prospect's need to improve their life and buy from you. What life improvement are they searching for? What pain are they wanting to move away from? What's the consequence if they don't do something about it?

Look at it this way. When you take your car into the shop for service, what happens? The mechanics don't immediately start working on your car the second you get there. They ask you questions about the problem, and then they hook up your car to a computer, and run a diagnostic test. Otherwise, they might start working on the engine when the problem was with the transmission. So, in order to tune up your prospects and yourself and fix what actually needs to be fixed, you need to use your own diagnostic tool. And that's your own curiosity.

Keith Krach is the groundbreaking founder of billion-dollar companies like DocuSign and Ariba. On June 20, 2019, he was unanimously confirmed by the U.S. Senate to serve under the Secretary of State for economical growth, energy, and environment. And Krach credits curiosity for much of his success.

On a fundamental level, Krach believes that a great salesperson is like a great doctor. No matter what you're selling, your job essentially has two general pathways. If the patient is visibly sick, it's the salesperson's job to convince that sick patient that they need the medicine they're prescribing to get better. If the patient is on a path that will lead them to illness, it's the salesperson's job to convince the patient that if they don't change their habits, and take their preventative medicine, that sickness is right around the corner.

But you can't diagnose the sickness if you don't have the curiosity to figure it out first.

The key to sales warrior curiosity is that it's targeted. It isn't about open-ended questions, or letting the prospect guide the conversation, it's about asking guiding questions that move the sale forward. And that means starting with the unsatisfied triple bind.

The greatest way to start the ball rolling on your curiosity, is also the first step of our 5 Steps to Understand Your Customer's Mission, the award-winning methodology we teach clients to gain position of strength in the first few minutes of the conversation.* And this starts with the unsatisfied triple bind.

Milton Erickson, the godfather of hypnosis therapy, used binding questions as a technique to subtly give prospects guided choices, where any of those three gives you your desired outcome. So this might sound like,

---

* Contact sales@FPG.com for more information about the 5 Steps to Understand Your Customer's Mission.

"The reason prospects choose us is because of blank, blank, and blank. Of those three things, which is most important to you?"

This is guided curiosity. You're not asking about the weather, or where they grew up, or even what they want right away. You're guiding the conversation by using your sales warrior curiosity, and that opens up even more questions as you go. This is true warrior curiosity.

I know that the more curious I am, the more successful I become.

One of the best ways I've found to overcome the fear of leaning into the prospect conversation, is to let your curiosity guide you. It will never steer you wrong.

APPLICATION

Curiosity is intentional, and it starts before you ever step into the arena with a prospect. You can engage your curiosity beforehand by experiencing that moment in your mind's eye, and understanding how it will benefit both you and your future customer.

By following this purpose, physiology, perspective exercise, you'll naturally engage your curiosity before the conversation even begins.

1. What is the purpose of your conversation with your prospect? What are you trying to accomplish? What is your ideal end result?

2. What will your physiology be with your prospect? How will you physically be positioned when you speak with them? Will you be standing, speaking to them in person? Will you be sitting, speaking to them over the phone? What is your energy level? Will you be excited? Speaking loudly? Softly?

3. Create your perspective. Close your eyes and visualize your sale. Step into the selling moment and see what you'll see in that moment. Feel what you'll feel in that moment. Hear what you'll hear in that moment. Consciously turn up the volume and brightness of the picture. Experience your curiosity in surround sound, and see yourself uncovering your prospect's problems with your never-ending curiosity.

4. Repeat this process any time you want to add more curiosity to your selling process.

25

DEMAND COACHING

"The level of my success is equal to the amount of coaching I demand."

Sales warriors don't just want coaching, or even ask for coaching, they **demand** coaching.

Your level of improvement is a direct result of your desire for coaching. It's pretty simple: how much you want coaching is directly tied to how much you want to improve. And to truly have the mindset of the sales warrior, you have to not just run toward coaching, you have to absolutely demand it. It's the fundamental difference between these two statements.

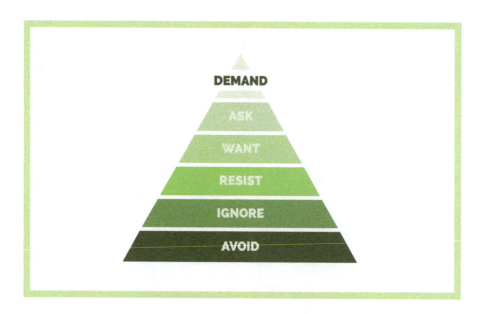

Asking: "I would love some coaching from you on this at some point."

Demanding: "I have a problem right now, and I absolutely need your perspective on it, so I can earn what I'm truly worth."

I ask coaches this question all the time: "What percentage of your employees are currently on a plateau?" Every time I ask this question, people usually say 20%, 50%, 70%. The answer is actually 100% *unless* they're demanding coaching, and that coach is responding by unleashing them with the strategies to earn what they're truly worth. That's the joy of a true coach-employee relationship.

The most common pushback against coaching that I hear from salespeople, is that they believe that by demanding coaching, they're somehow admitting that they're broken. Or, that they have no clue what they're doing. There's some negative programming there that deserves exploring, but on a base level, that's not at all what demanding coaching is about.

Tim Grover has been the personal trainer to some of the most elite athletes, including names like Michael Jordan, Kobe Bryant, Dwayne Wade, and Charles Barkley. In Grover's book, *Relentless*, he outlines the 13 things that extremely successful people do. He describes their mindset and work ethic, and how those two areas make them unstoppable.

Specifically, he explains how winners fall into one of these three categories: Cooler, a Closer, or a Cleaner.

A **Cooler** is careful. They wait to be told what to do, they watch to see what everyone else is up to, and they follow the leader. They are mediators, not decision makers. Coolers can handle a certain amount of pressure when things are going well, but when the heat turns up, they kick the problem over to someone else. In other words, they set others up for success.

A **Closer** can handle tons of pressure and gets the job done. If you put a closer in the right situation and tell them what to do, they'll do it. Closers are powered by attention and validation. The Closer is the ultimate competitor, the person you can count on to finish the game or make a deal. They simply do what they are supposed to do, receive that credit, and go home happy.

A **Cleaner**, on the other hand, is relentless. They're never satisfied, and constantly create new goals every time they reach their personal best. They thrive under pressure, make decisions instead of suggestions, and know who they are. If you're good, you keep going until you're great. If you're great, it means you fight until you're unstoppable. Cleaners, in other words, are sales warriors.

Something else Cleaners do? They demand excellence, they demand positive results, and they demand coaching.

The point is that a good coach will help you find things in yourself that you *didn't even know were there*. Sometimes the coach will find it for you, but sometimes they'll give you the tools so you can find it in *yourself*. That's what great coaching does. It fills you with the self-confidence and internal motivation to unleash yourself, and that leads to a life of continuous, never-ending improvement.

In my book, *Leadership Sales Coaching*[*], I define the purpose of a coach as a person you follow to a place you wouldn't go on your own.

Your coaches will value the demand for coaching as well. Studies show that one of the greatest indicators of success, is someone's desire for improvement. By displaying that need for growth to your coach, you aren't just helping yourself. You're letting your light shine to your peers that you don't just want growth; you demand it.

So, if you have any internal oppositional reflex to subconsciously reject coaching, you need to create a miracle for yourself. If you believe, "My coach doesn't have time for me," or, "There's nothing my coach can do to help me", then you need to change the way you view coaching. You need to realize that coaching is happening *for* you, not *to* you. And if your coach outright refuses to coach you, then you need to demand it from somewhere else. The way a true Cleaner would.

Great coaching isn't about fixing what's broken, it's about helping you see that you were never broken all along and liberating you from the leashes that hold you back.

APPLICATION

Whenever you've thought about where you'll be in a year, you've probably always seen this future through your own eyes. I'm willing to bet that every time you imagined your future, you associate it with who you are now, which blocks who you could be.

Cognitive behavioral therapists will often have their patients who experienced a trauma detach from their "first person" views and feelings in order to gain perspective, by viewing the situation from a third person viewpoint.

In order to do that, you are going to disassociate from your current self and time travel one year into the future. Be sure to share this with your coach.

1. **Identify where you are right now.** Where are you in your career? What is the most important thing to you right now? Don't think about where you are going, think about you right now in this very moment. Write all of this down on a piece of paper.

2. **Disassociate.** Now you're going to time travel one year into the future from the perspective of an outsider. In order to do this, close your eyes and imagine you're no longer you. You're an outsider looking at a new character from a third person viewpoint. Where is this character? What have they accomplished? What characteristics does this person have? What did this person do to be where they are today? Write it all down as specifically as possible.

3. **Plan.** What did this character have that you don't right now? What did they do to get from where they were, to where they are? How do their values and characteristics compare to yours at this moment? What do you need to change right now in order to become this person? Write it all down.

Disassociative coaching takes practice, but once you grasp the concept, you can do it very quickly in any situation that would normally cause you to freeze and feel helpless. This skill will allow you to coach yourself away from your own leashing emotions, so you can grow yourself into a better version of you.

26

BUILD UP YOUR INNER VOICE

> **I only use my inner voice to build myself up.**

One of the most impactful speeches of all time is Steve Jobs' commencement address to the Stanford class of 2005. During his speech, he delivered this powerful line: **"Don't let the noise of others' opinions drown out your inner voice."**

During every moment of every day, we carry on an inner dialogue that guides our actions, and shapes how we see the world around us.

Scientists from the Netherlands conducted a study around the inner voice. They watched women struggling with anorexia walk through doorways in a lab. They noticed that the women physically turned their shoulders sideways to squeeze through the doors, even though they had plenty of room. They concluded that the inner voices of these women were so strong that their internal representations of themselves actually determined their body's movements. Their inner voice told them what they were, and they behaved based on those voices-even though the reality was completely different.

In other words, their inner voice dictated their actions.

Your inner voice is a powerful tool that will lead you to your goals, but sometimes the opinions of others can become louder. We've all worried about the opinions of others at one point or another. Maybe you've fallen victim to the opinions of your prospects, your coworkers, or even your spouse. But if we listen to those opinions instead of our own voice, we're quickly misled from the path towards our goals.

In fact, your inner voice is so powerful that it can actually trigger brain activity. If you're told to visualize something, the parts of your brain associated with vision light up. Just the same, your inner voice can also trigger negative reactions. Researchers recently discovered something called the nocebo effect. The placebo effect is when you're given a sugar pill, told it has positive effects, and suddenly you start to feel better. The nocebo effect is the opposite; give someone a sugar pill but tell them about the negative side effects instead of the positive.

Guess what happens? They start exhibiting those negative side effects. Their self-talk is reinforcing the negative input from the outside. If you're told that a negative side effect to a surgery is pain in a certain area, then you are clinically more likely to feel pain in that area.

You need to unplug yourself from the problem before it becomes a full-fledged leash. When you unplug from something, you mentally remove yourself from damaging outside opinions you want to avoid, and plug into the beneficial inner voice that counters those negative outside thoughts or beliefs.

I want you to imagine a scenario. You're about to hop on a sales call with a decision-maker. You're nervous, but you know this is a chance to close a major account. Before the call, you're milling around in the break room and a coworker says to you, "Man, I'm glad I'm not making that call, that guy rips apart everyone he talks to. I've heard selling that guy is impossible."

How might you react to that? You might shrug it off on the outside, but mentally your brain starts going haywire. Your inner voice starts to panic, and now you're doubting yourself, your selling process, and everything in between. You're saying things to yourself like, "There's no way I can do this," and, "I might as well not even make the call." That bleeds into the call itself. Now you sound nervous, falter on your process, and the sale goes down the tubes.

This is an example of how outer voices influence inner voices, and how inner voices influence results.

The first step is understanding what your self-talk is. Are you talking yourself out of deals because your inner voice is downgrading your abilities? Or, are you building yourself up with motivating statements that give you the best possible chance to succeed?

Your inner voice controls so much about your actions. No matter what you're doing, you're either telling yourself goal-preventing statements, or goal-supporting self-talk statements. Here are examples of both.

A goal-preventing statement is an excuse. It negatively programs your mindset to keep you away from achieving your goals. A goal-preventing statement sounds like, "I can't follow up right now because most people have Monday morning meetings."

A goal supporting statement on the other hand, will only bring you positive results. Goal supporting statements refocus your mindset towards your goals, and positively program you for success. A goal-supporting statement sounds like, "I want to be the first person to talk to them this week, and if I miss them, I'll call back later today."

Here are six criteria to identify goal-supporting self-talk from from *The Psychology of Sales Call Reluctance*, by George W. Dudley and Shannon L. Goodson.

1. **Is it true?**

   Who else would believe this statement? Can you find facts and statistics that support this statement? If you were to say this statement to a close friend or colleague, and they didn't believe it, chances are you're not using goal supporting self-talk.

2. **Is it consistent?**

   Is your self-talk aligned with your goals? Are you using positive language that pushes you towards making sales? Or, is your language pulling your progress back further? When your self-talk is consistent with your goals, you're positively programming your mindset, and that leads to more sales.

3. **Is it positive?**

   Optimistic thoughts such as "I have the ability to make this sale", or, "My purpose is to improve lives" can keep negative thoughts at bay. If your self-talk is clouded with pessimistic statements, your behavior will reflect that, and your sales will tank.

4. **Is it unbiased?**

   Do you find that your self-talk sounds like an enemy inside your head pointing out your every flaw? If so, you need to reprogram your self-talk into an objective voice that focuses on facts without personal opinions. When your inner voice is objective, it becomes your guide towards success.

5. **Is it freeing?**

   Does your self-talk add to your anxiety and stress? Or does it release you from your fear, and inspire you to run towards your goals? Your self-talk needs to unleash you from your doubts so you can lead your sales fearlessly.

6. **Is it enriching?**

   Your self-talk is like your guide in a forest. It should always serve as a light out of darkness, rather than make your surroundings darker.

Your self-talk should always provide you with positive perspectives during uncertainty or challenges you face.

If the words your inner self is saying to you don't meet these criteria, then your self-talk is actively working against you.

The key to turning around destructive self-talk, is to fight the fire with affirmation statements. It's to turn back those negative words and replace them with positives. Just start with simple statements that affirm what you already know to be true. Tell yourself things like, "I have everything within me now to be successful," or, "I was built for this moment." The effect these statements have on your state of mind will be immediately evident in the way you come across. And the fun thing about confident inner dialogue, is that it turns into confident outer dialogue.

All of us have internal affirmations every minute of every day. You're constantly affirming your ability, your beliefs, your capabilities, your successes, your setbacks. The key is to identify which affirmations are helping you, and which are harming you, and that takes forethought.

Affirmations help you create that forethought by programming your subconscious. Forethought sounds like this: "My goal is that I want my prospect to feel relaxed and at ease, and have resolution, and therefore I want to present three simple options, and state them in positive ways, so they're easily understood". Then that becomes the affirmation: "I am a sales warrior who always presents three options that always allows the prospect to feel relaxed and brings them to resolution."

Do this consciously and you'll have the self-talk of a sales warrior.

APPLICATION

Your mind is a powerful tool. It allows you to manifest your ideas into reality when those ideas are supported by your own beliefs and behaviors.

Use these eight criteria, developed by The Pacific Institute, to create your affirmations.

1. It's personal. Start with "I" or "me."

2. It's positive. Use uplifting language.

3. It's present tense. Don't make it something you've done, or will do.

4. It indicates achievement. Use "I am", or "I do", not "I can", "I will", "I want", or "I should".

5. It uses action words ("quickly", "easily", "fluidly") and emotion words ("proud", "enthusiastic").

6. It's specific and detailed.

7. It's confident.

8. It's realistic.

Say this statement 3 times a day, for the next 90 days. If needed, program reminders into your phone to alert you to speak your affirming statement every day.

27

ONE STEP, ONE DECISION, ONE PROSPECT AT A TIME

"When I focus on the process, the score takes care of itself."

As far as my personality goes, I'm a process-driven person. But that doesn't mean that I'm locked into a robotic routine, where every step I take is somehow automated beyond my control. I own my process, and because I own my process, I also own the direction it goes. Once I've found a process that leads me to success, I lock onto it because I know it works, and takes uncertainty and anxiety out of the equation.

When it comes to following a process, nobody does it quite as well as top level athletes.

I believe that salespeople are corporate athletes, and in order for them to achieve peak performance, they need to be treated as such. That doesn't mean running laps around the building (although regular walks do help productivity), but it does mean doing the things a corporate athlete does. And the biggest learning we can pick up from the sports world, is the idea that following a process will change everything for you.

That's the heart of the idea behind **One Step, One Decision, One Prospect at a Time**.

If you're a baseball fan, you probably know about David Ortiz. Ortiz was one of the best players of all time, and he's one of the greatest examples of the importance of taking a process and chunking it down for maximum follow through.

Every time he stepped up to the plate, he broke down his process and practiced his techniques separately, so he was always prepared for anything the pitcher threw. He had a process for every batting practice, for every at-bat, for every type of pitcher. He studied. He learned. He practiced. Because of his ability to chunk down his hitting skills into a step-by-step process, he became one of the best ever. And because he had a process, he was able to make small course corrections all along the way. He knew if a right-handed pitcher always threw in one direction, he could look for tells about when it was about to happen.

Going forward, I want this to be your mantra as a sales warrior: **One Step, One Decision, One Prospect at a Time**. No matter what you're doing, you have to chunk it down to the smallest possible step so you can avoid feeling overwhelmed by the circumstances around you. When you feel overwhelmed, the brain essentially shuts down. It stops regulating a chemical called cortisol, which controls things like your energy level, how well you sleep, and your blood pressure. So, you feel drained, your immune system doesn't work properly, and you're more likely to get headaches and experience anxiety.

So how do you avoid all that? You chunk it down. Every time you think, "There's nothing I can do about the economy," I want you to say to yourself,

"One Step, One Decision, One Prospect at a Time." Every time you say, "I can't control my prospects' decisions," I want you to think, **"One Step, One Decision, One Prospect at a Time."** Every time it seems like the market is getting worse, I want you to feel, **"One Step, One Decision, One Prospect at a Time."**

Internationally bestselling author, Haruki Murakami, had this to say about the importance of sticking to his process:

> "When I'm in writing mode for a novel, I get up at 4 a.m. and work for five to six hours. In the afternoon, I run for 10 kilometers or swim for 1,500 meters (or do both), then I read a bit and listen to some music. I go to bed at 9 p.m. I keep to this routine every day without variation. The repetition itself becomes the important thing; it's a form of mesmerism. I mesmerize myself to reach a deeper state of mind."

The key piece here, is that the repetition of a process unlocked a deeper state of productivity and focus. When your process becomes second nature, any anxiety or nerves you have around selling can disappear. Your process will free your mind so you can focus on moving the sale forward.

The point is that processes aren't robotic. They don't lock you into a state where you're suddenly not *you*. That couldn't be further from the truth. A sales warrior realizes that a process in the course of the sale is the *only* way to truly let their own light shine.

Give yourself the gift of a process, focus on one step at a time within that process, and let the score take care of itself. Study the processes adopted by top 1% sales warriors. Learn about why they were successful. Commit yourself to following them. Understand the big picture, but don't focus on it. Instead, focus on the steps to make that picture come true. You'll be amazed at the results when you're focused on the brushstrokes, not the painting itself.

APPLICATION

Taking everything one step at a time can be a challenge when tasks pile up and the to-do list gets overwhelming. But that's exactly the right time to change your mantra to **"One Step, One Decision, One Prospect at a Time."** Turn your wide-angle lens into a pinpoint-focused camera so you can achieve anything you want to achieve.

1. Write down a prospect you want to close right now.

2. Chunk it down. Make a list of all the decisions the prospect needs to make in order to choose you. Notice as you do this that your anxiety decreases.

3. Focus on one step, one decision at a time. As you accomplish more and more steps in the process, fight the urge to zoom out on the battlefield. Stay locked into the next step in your process. Do this in every circumstance going forward, both in your sales and in your personal life.

28

HAVE NO FEAR

> "I sell every prospect as if I'm permanently dead."

The Japanese Samurai would meditate about their own deaths every morning and every night. They envisioned themselves dying in hundreds of different ways, every single day, without fail.

Even if the practice seems morbid to us today, the outcome was psychologically important. They meditated about their deaths because if they imagined they were already dead, they could no longer be afraid of their own death. They became fearless in battle and were able to live in the moment with perfect bravery.

In other words, if they took away the fear of death within their own minds, nobody else could lord that over them. They removed that power from anyone else, and it allowed them to live fearlessly. It was never *really* about death at all. It was about personal empowerment.

Modern research backs this up. Reflecting on death can actually be a powerful vehicle for self-improvement in the present. A study by psychologist, Adam Grant, found that when people are reminded of their mortality, they become more productive and purposeful. In essence, they've removed the reactive tendency to be fearful.

There's a concept I use all the time called the "no monster". Every salesperson has this intimidating vision of the word "no" in their head, to the point that it becomes an unconquerable monster. But really, "no" is just a word. And, if you think about it, it's not a scary word either.

"EVERY TIME YOU GO INTO A SELLING SITUATION, YOU HAVE TO BELIEVE THAT YOU'LL NEVER HAVE ANOTHER CONVERSATION WITH THAT PROSPECT."

What would happen if you viewed every "no", as a "not yet"? They just don't have enough value built up around what you sell. They don't fully understand *why*, or *how*, you're about to change their life yet. There's never a reason to fear "no" if you hear the objection as, "I need you to keep selling me so I can truly understand how you're about to remove the pain I have right now, and guide me toward life improvement."

What would *that* do for your sales results?

Brandon Steiner is the founder of Steiner Sports, one of the most influential sports memorabilia companies in the world. Steiner staked his reputation on being bold. Before one pitch meeting, he found out the decision-maker's favorite sport was running, bought him a pair of new running shoes, and only sent him the left shoe with a letter attached: "Tomorrow when I come in and meet with you, we're going to get off on the right foot." He showed up the next day with the right shoe, and he closed the deal that day.

That's how you sell as if you're permanently dead.

At its core, this idea of becoming permanently dead is fundamentally about freedom. It's about freeing yourself from the tyranny of your fear, which chains you from your own progress. If you're disproportionately afraid of death, you'll recoil from any activity that seems like a threat to that fear. At that level, even the morning commute produces fear-based anxiety. And that limits your happiness. Just the same, salespeople often have dozens of fears running through their minds at any given moment. "What if I ask for the sale and they say 'no'?" "What if they don't like my selling message?" "What if they don't care what I have to say?"

What if. What if. What if.

The purpose of becoming permanently dead to your fears is to quiet all those what-ifs. The Samurai lived as though they were permanently dead to eliminate the fear of death. You can borrow this idea of becoming permanently dead to eliminate whatever fears are leashing you from selling like you were born to sell.

The way you do this, is to simply sell as if you have nothing to lose. Because guess what? You don't. I make it a goal to walk into every selling situation with the mindset that I have nothing to fear. I tell myself, "I am strengthened by the word no". This liberates me from the leashes that keep me from helping people improve their lives. Because when I give into my fears, I'm also limiting my ability to help others. How often has that happened to you?

This has to be a total mindset shift from your current reality, but it's entirely possible. Every time you go into a selling situation, you have to believe that you'll never have another conversation with that prospect. You have to believe that there will never be another opportunity for you to make your pitch, to say that one more thing you needed to say to convince the prospect. How would that change your message? How would that add urgency to your push to improve their life?

This concept is relevant in just about every facet of modern life. In sports, you hear coaches and players tell each other to "leave it all on the field." In life, we often say, "live life like there's no tomorrow."

Your goal at the end of every day is to be able to look in the mirror and convincingly tell yourself, "I did everything I could've done today to move the sale forward." If not? You weren't selling as if you were permanently dead.

So what keeps salespeople from becoming sales warriors in this area? It's fear. It's overthinking the result of what *might happen* if they put themselves out there and it all goes wrong. In reality, that's a mental hijack.

Fear is nothing more than a state of excitement, and all excitement produces the same reactions in your body. Your heart rate increases, you breathe a little quicker, and your palms begin to sweat. Your reaction to being chased in the woods by a bear produces the same physiological response as if you were surprised with a check for a million dollars. The only difference between fear and excitement, is your attitude about it.

When you reframe your perspective about fear, it becomes a positive state of excitement. And that's how you sell as though you're permanently dead.

APPLICATION

It's time to remove your "no monster".

The best way to overcome any fear of the word "no" you may have, is to build up your knowledge of the life-changing value you provide to your prospects. Follow the steps below to eradicate your "no monster", and shift your view of "no", to "not yet".

1. Write out a list of as many ways you improve peoples' lives as possible. How are you saving them from pain? What will happen to them if they *don't* choose you?

2. Take time each day to reflect on one of these areas. See, feel, and hear in your mind's eye what will happen to a prospect if they don't choose you, and fail to achieve their goals.

3. Pull from this list any time you feel fear around hearing the word "no." Lean on your value, and how you alone can lead your prospect to true life improvement any time the "no monster" threatens your results.

29

MORE CONFLICT, MORE CHANGE

" I am strengthened by conflict. "

Change comes from growth, and growth comes from conflict. Think about all the life lessons you hold close to you. They probably all emerged from some kind of struggle that you've experienced in your life. As painful as those moments are, you're stronger and smarter because of them.

It's like when you try a new workout program, and the first few weeks are rough. You can barely move because you're so sore, and each new exercise sets your muscles on fire. But then you notice that the more you're pushing yourself, the more you change. You no longer toss and turn through the night, you have a long-lasting energy throughout the day, and you actually look forward to each new workout because you know that the challenge is making you stronger.

Conflict doesn't hinder us, it strengthens us.

Salespeople are afraid of conflict. Sales warriors know that, without conflict, there is no change. Every prospect who's interested in buying from you will have some sort of objection. One thing I know is that the prospects you speak with who don't have objections almost definitely aren't going to buy from you. Objections are just a natural part of the buying process; it's a sign your prospect is actively working through it in their mind, and that's exactly what you want. That's why sales warriors aren't just prepared for conflict, they welcome it.

"THE MORE OBJECTIONS YOU HEAR, THE CLOSER YOU ARE TO CLOSING THE SALE."

Objections are nothing more than feedback, and the more objections you hear, the closer you are to closing the sale. So often salespeople think of objections as criticism, and I've even seen some take a prospect's objections personally.

As a sales warrior you should not only welcome feedback, but you should revere it. Feedback is the path to mastery. You can't remove your prospect's leashes unless you have the knowledge first. You can't handle your buyer's objections until you know what they are. Imagine the certainty you'll have when you know exactly what's holding the buyer back from choosing you, over all alternatives. That's what having no fear of conflict is all about.

All the time, I see salespeople procrastinate on this step because they've been programmed to see conflict as negative. Always remember this:

Conflict isn't a negative in the hands of a sales warrior who wants to improve their prospects' lives. Productive conflict is absolutely the fastest way to close the sale.

In recent years, psychologists have become aware of the phenomenon known as "post conflict growth". This term was coined by Richard Tedeschi and Lawrence Calhoun, who interviewed dozens of people who experienced traumatic life events. They found that for many of these people, dealing with this huge traumatic conflict released a surge of personal development and growth. It wasn't just a coping skill, they actually gained significant benefits from it. In Tedeschi and Calhoun's terms, they experienced "positive life changes". They gained new inner strength, and often developed skills and abilities that they never knew they had before.

The exciting part of conflict is that it's the way to achieve resolution with the prospect that can't be achieved any other way. When you view conflict as a win/win, and not a win/lose proposition, you immediately go from feeling weak to feeling strong.

Instead of viewing conflict as a battle between you and the prospect, it's really an internal struggle the prospect is going through on their own. They want to take the next step and make a purchase, but they're going through an internal war. "Should I buy? Should I not buy? Should I buy from here? Or here? What features do I need? How will I know when I've found the right one?"

When you see it like this, you can truly view yourself as their vehicle for life improvement. You can help them win that internal battle they're having with themselves by providing solutions. And best of all, it helps you truly understand where their frustration comes from. When it bubbles up to the surface in the form of indecision or confusion, it isn't personal. It's just part of their personal conflict that you can help them solve.

Conflict is all about achieving a breakthrough for your prospects. The process isn't just empowering, exciting, and necessary, it's also the kind of conflict that they will thank you for the rest of their lives.

APPLICATION

Box breathing is a technique that Navy SEALs use to get their minds in the proper state to face conflict. The best part, is that it's simple. You can use it anywhere, from the privacy of your own home, to the most public place. So, when you're feeling anxiety in a tough moment, and are struggling to embrace conflict, use this strategy to stabilize yourself and become ready for the moment. You'll find that as you follow these steps over time, you'll become more and more at ease with any conflict situations.

Just follow these steps.

1. Sit with your back supported in a comfortable chair and with your feet on the floor.

2. With your eyes closed, breathe in through your nose while counting to four slowly.

3. Feeling the air enter your lungs, hold your breath inside your lungs for four seconds.

4. Slowly exhale through your mouth for four seconds.

5. Keep your lungs free from air for four seconds.

6. Repeat steps 2 through 5 until you're in a calm state, and your mind is clear of distractions.

30

I AM ENOUGH

"When I realize that I am enough, I become unstoppable."

Brené Brown became a viral sensation almost overnight when her TED Talk, "The Power of Vulnerability," hit the mainstream. Brown's message was simple: in order for true connection to happen, we have to allow our real selves to be truly seen by others, and that requires vulnerability.

What she found by researching the effects of vulnerability and shame, is people who have a strong sense of internal worthiness and external belonging believe they deserve it. That's it. Sales warriors who have a strong internal mindset and a strong sense of their external identity in the broader sales tribe just feel they're worthy of those things. It's all mindset.

And the way you feel worthy of it is by embodying the phrase Brown says at the very end of her talk, which quickly became the foundation for my own company.

"When I believe I'm enough, I stop screaming and I start listening."

What a message. Salespeople "scream" in the form of alibis and excuses, which sounds like, "I don't have enough willing buyers," or, "I have no support from my team." What happens when you scream? You don't listen to coaching. You don't listen to feedback. You don't listen to your prospects. You don't listen to anybody, including your own inner voice. In other words, you stop your growth entirely.

This screaming is a result of a belief system that says, "I'm not enough." They've been denied vulnerability somewhere along the way, and so their programming is now shame-based. Shame says, "I *am* the mistake." That's a deeply-held belief that you're somehow broken, and the result of your setbacks is somehow based on your identity as a person. Again, this comes from a programmed "I'm not enough" mentality. This is looking at a lost sale as some deeply moral failing within yourself, not as a learning experience detached from your own sense of worthiness. If you truly believed your setbacks define you, then you also believe that there's nothing you can do to improve. You're stuck.

Guilt, on the other hand, can be a healthy motivator. Guilt says, "I *made* a mistake." See the difference? That disassociates you from the root of the problem. Now you have something tangible you can improve, as opposed to internalizing and embodying the problem within yourself.

This is the core of vulnerability as a sales warrior. When you believe you're enough, now you're actively listening to others and yourself. Now you have open arms to coaching, to improvement, to true internal growth. Now you've rejected shame entirely.

If you get nothing else from this book, get this: you are worthy. You are enough to achieve anything you want to achieve. You are enough to reach that sales goal that someone told you was impossible. You are enough to close any sale at any moment.

And above all else, you are enough to become the sales warrior you were born to be.

APPLICATION

Positive disagreement is the process of taking a negative you currently believe about yourself or your abilities, and turning it around into a positive. In essence, you're inserting doubt into your process and questioning whether you truly believe that negative thought, or whether it was implanted there.

This is the path to replacing those "I'm not enough" statements with an "I am enough" mindset.

1. Write out five negative beliefs about your current circumstances that are holding you back right now. (Example: "I'm in a slump.")

2. Rewrite those negative beliefs as though the opposing belief is the truth. (Example: Next to "I'm in a slump," write, "I'm on the edge of a breakthrough.")

3. Focus on making these positive disagreement statements your new "I am enough" mantras. For every negative belief or thought you have about your current abilities or circumstances, create a positive disagreement, and adopt that as your new belief.

31

GRATITUDE IS COURAGE

"Gratitude is the unyielding fuel for courage."

If you want more courage in your life, all you need to do is add more gratitude.

When my company won its first best place to work award, I was thrilled. I'd built FPG on the belief that a great culture drives great performance, and to see that belief externally validated with an award was an achievement that caused me to swell up with pride. So when we arrived at the venue to find out our place, I was practically riding on a cloud.

And then I heard our place: Ninth.

In that moment, I was devastated. *Ninth?* My belief system was built around the idea that we were the best place to work in America. We should've been first. How did this happen? As I stewed on this fact with my arms crossed, not understanding how we didn't have a higher ranking, I looked around at my team. They were *thrilled*. They were high-fiving, cheering, pumping their fists. And here I was, pouting like a kid who didn't get what they wanted on Christmas.

In that moment, I realized something: I was focused on perfection, not excellence. Perfection, is an unattainable standard that produces feelings of inadequacy. Excellence, is the belief that I will always be better than I was yesterday. And a mindset focused on incremental growth and excellence produces gratitude, and gratitude produces courage.

Instead of having gratitude for what we'd accomplished, I was focused on my perfectionism, which centered me on what I *hadn't* accomplished.

Think about the effect this has on your sales. There will always be things you *didn't* accomplish, just like there will always be things you *did* accomplish. So you have a choice. You can focus on the first category and feel small, or focus on the second category and feel big. If you make yourself feel big, you'll do big things. Just the same, if you make yourself feel small, you'll do small things.

This isn't an idle strategy. The entire purpose is to make this moment about gratitude, so your next moment can be about gratitude. If I'd stayed in that place of perfectionism, we'd have never made the list the next year. Or the year after that, or the year after that (which we did). Instead, I chose to follow my team's lead, and see it through a lens of gratitude. I focused on the strategies we took to get us there, and that gave me the courage to see ways we could make our culture even better. And that's exactly what happened.

The health benefits of gratitude are beyond question. Among other benefits, it improves your physical and psychological health, it increases your self-esteem, and it gives you more mental strength. But I believe the biggest reason why gratitude will change everything for you, is because it gives you the courage you need to achieve your goals.

And the best news? You can go back to your own personal gratitude well whenever you need. If you need courage to make that next sales presentation, just pull from a time in your past when you succeeded, and pull gratitude from that moment. If you need courage to have a tough conversation with your boss, just pull from a time in your past when you achieved resolution through a tough conversation, and pull gratitude from that moment.

It's all linked. Whenever you need more courage, just have more gratitude.

APPLICATION

Your gratitude begins with awareness around what you have to be grateful for. Your entire life is one long list of gratitude moments that you can use to fuel your courage for any obstacle you face in your life.

The point is to recognize the areas where you achieved a desired result in your life, and then use those strategies to bring that success forward. The more gratitude you have for your successes, and the more awareness you have around what you did to achieve them, the more confidence you'll have moving forward.

Creating your gratitude lifeline is your first step on this journey.

1. Write out specific instances over the course of your life when you achieved success.

2. Write out the 5 most common steps you utilized to achieve these results.

3. Bring forward these strategies for your future goals.

32

THE GROWTH MINDSET

> " I get better with every new strategy I learn. "

Only positive change comes from adding more resources.

If you want a mantra to live by, you can't get much better than this Neuro-Linguistic Programming (NLP) presupposition about the human condition. So often we think of new strategies and new learnings as a burden: "Here comes another thing I have to figure out." But in reality, your brain only has one response when you add a new strategy: it grows.

In Carol Dweck's groundbreaking book, *Mindset*, she defines two types of mental states: the growth mindset and the fixed mindset.

A fixed mindset believes in static programming. This is a helpless way of thinking; it believes there's no way to improve or grow beyond where you are today. This is the voice telling you, "I've arrived. I know everything I need to know in order to be the best salesperson I can possibly be." At that point you've cut the line between your present self and your future self. You'll never grow again.

The growth mindset, on the other hand, is focused on continual learning and improvement. It means constantly challenging self-programming by pushing the boundaries of what's possible, and if that programming isn't beneficial, it's examined and then thrown away. It means seeing a new process as a chance to become better, not as another thing to throw onto the to-do list.

I find that the more I learn about selling, the more I realize how little I truly know. And you know what? That's an invigorating thought for me. There's so much left to learn, so many areas where I can still grow. That's life fuel, not just for me, but for you as well.

"WE TRAIN IN TIMES OF PEACE SO WE DON'T GET BLOODY IN WAR."

Your mindset determines everything about you as a sales warrior, and your mindset comes from how you've been programmed to think. The good news is that you can change your programming. But first you have to change your mindset, and that starts with a growth mindset.

One thing I know about sales warriors, is that they have that authentic growth mindset. They're surrounding themselves with development opportunities and people who will encourage that development. They challenge programming that holds them back from achieving more. And most importantly, they have reality thinking around how they've been programmed to think.

It's easy to chase a growth mindset when it's obvious you need to grow. But the most convenient lie salespeople tell themselves, is that they don't need to grow and improve because they're already high producers. This is where it helps to see things like a Navy SEAL.

The SEALs, one of the most elite military units in the world, live by this mantra: "We train in times of peace so we don't get bloody in war."

I've seen too many sales careers end because they didn't embody this message, because they weren't prepared for the next bad economy, the next slow sales month, the next company restructuring. One thing we know about the economy is that it's cyclical, and that on average it takes a nosedive every seven years or so. If you know that you're at the apex of a booming economy, then you know that the downward fall is right around the corner.

There's only one joy greater than the joy of success, and that's the joy of growth. That's because growth lasts longer. You can achieve your goal for the year, but on January 1st, that goal resets. It's old news. If you add a new strategy, or a new selling resource, that improvement will last you the rest of your life. You can do it every day, regardless of the circumstances.

The joy of a growth mindset is your floatation device as a sales warrior. Use it, lean on it, love it.

APPLICATION

Your growth mindset as a sales warrior isn't arrived organically. It's a process that requires time, repetition and mindfulness. Because of that, you need to create that mindset within you now, and this process will help you do that.

Find yourself on this growth mindset scale. The more aware you are of your own mindset and abilities, and the more you rely on the strategies you find in this book, the closer to number four you'll be 100% of the time. And that's how you know you have a growth mindset.

So, on a scale of one to four...

1. I have a certain amount of talent in sales, and I can't do much to change it.

2. I can learn new things, but I can't really change how talented I am in sales.

3. No matter how much talent I have in me, I can usually change it quite a bit.

4. I can always substantially change how talented I am in sales.

What in your life do you need to see differently in order to level up? To achieve a growth mindset, your focus should be on your ability to follow the process of working towards a higher level of consciousness versus just focusing on the success itself.

33

LIVE IN REALITY

" I always see things as they are, not better or worse than they are. "

A true reality mindset comes when your inner understanding matches the outer circumstances. Anything other than that, is just deceptive thinking.

Markets change all the time, which means circumstances are constantly rising and falling; one minute they're in your favor, the next they're not. When circumstances are easy, that's when you'll get things called market sales. These don't require much convincing or extra effort. When you speak with prospects, they're already on the brink of buying, they're just deciding on their final options. Conversion rates tend to climb in these seasons.

And then, you have down markets, when you speak with fewer prospects who are ready to buy. Again, the natural arc is that sales decline as the potential pool of buyers thin out. Or, so most salespeople think.

The problem isn't the circumstance, it's the mindset surrounding the circumstance. When the market is great, salespeople fall victim to deceptive thinking. They don't recognize the market's role in their sales, so they coast, thinking they've got it all figured out. Then, when the winter economy hits, their sales plummet. This is the other side of the deceptive thinking boomerang: "It's not my fault my sales are down. It's the economy," they complain.

"SALES WARRIORS DON'T JUST MAINTAIN THEIR PACE WHEN THE WINTER ECONOMY HITS; THEY INCREASE IT."

The true sales warrior mindset is completely different. They see everything as happening for them, not to them. Instead, think, "My goal, regardless of the circumstances, is to maximize every opportunity." This means understanding which direction the wind is blowing and adjusting your sail accordingly. If you have the wind at your back, it's about maximizing the great weather. If you have the wind in your face, then it's about maximizing your strategies so you don't lose speed.

If your mindset is currently, "Of course my sales will drop when the market gets worse," then you're not thinking like a sales warrior. Because sales warriors don't just maintain their pace when the winter economy hits; they increase it.

So, let's say last month you spoke with 20 prospects, and this month you'll only speak with 10. You have two options in that moment. The first door is self-defeating. You could complain about the circumstances, and assume your sales will decrease because your potential buyer base has been cut in half. This is the door I've seen all too many salespeople take, and their burnout rate is astronomically higher than their peers.

Or, you could choose to simply see things as they are. Now you can spend more time with the prospects you speak with, and give them more time to see the value you can offer them. The point is that you're constantly re-coaching yourself to not inflate the negativity (or the positivity) of the moment you're in. The minute you do that, you've given up your control to the circumstance, and that's devastating for your sales.

Your mind is naturally trying to protect you at all times, but it actually works against you when it comes to having realistic thinking around extreme circumstances. When things are bad, your brain starts looking for threats; this is why you start looking outside yourself for reasons. When things are good, your brain is attempting to reward you. The most important thing for you, is to moderate both of those reactions.

That's why reality thinking is so important. By programming yourself to see the world as it is, and not how it might appear, you're taking another step on your journey to becoming the sales warrior.

APPLICATION

When you're able to expand your emotional vocabulary, you'll be better suited to understanding the reality of your circumstances, which will allow you to better shape your mindset for success. When you change your words, you'll change your emotions.

Researcher, Lisa Barrett, found that you can heighten your emotional intelligence by increasing your emotion vocabulary. For instance, if you say that an economy is "terrible," what is the frame of reference for that? Is it really terrible? Are there worse economies? Is there a more realistic word you can use? The word "terrible" programs you in a certain way, but if you can be more emotionally specific and say it's "more challenging than last quarter" Or, "more uncertain than last year", That's a different game.

1. Build out your emotional intelligence word list. Pick five of these words and commit to inserting them into your vocabulary to more accurately describe the circumstances around you, from prospects, to the economy, to your results, and everything in between.

   - Distracted
   - Expectant
   - Withdrawn
   - Confident
   - Confused
   - Victimized
   - Vibrant
   - Anxious
   - Enthusiastic
   - Frustrated
   - Paralyzed
   - Indifferent
   - Optimistic

2. As you continue to more accurately describe your circumstances, notice that your mindset around them becomes more realistic, less generalized, and gives you more empowerment. Commit to adding more, and more, emotionally specific words to give yourself the gift of increasing emotional intelligence.

34

LOCK ON

> "I choose to lock onto things that benefit me and lock out things that hold me back."

Part of your brainstem is called the Reticular Activating System. This is the physical part of the brain right at the base, and it's like your brain's gatekeeper for information. There is so much going on around you constantly that the Reticular Activating System (RAS) acts as the screen door to your consciousness. It decides what you notice, and what you don't notice.

Let's say you're in the market for a new car, and you spend hours researching that one car model. All of the sudden, you start seeing that car model everywhere: on your way to work, on the weekends, parked in your neighborhood. That's your RAS at work. Whether you realize it, or not, all that car research programmed your brain.

Your RAS is commonly known as the "goal-seeking mechanism" within your brain. Based on things you focus on, your RAS basically decides to lock onto what it thinks is important based on what you focus on, and shut out, or ignore, everything else. These are called "scotomas," a Greek word that means "blind spots". If you're not conscious about what your RAS is doing, your mind will naturally lock onto whatever it believes is most beneficial for your wellbeing, and it will blind you to everything else.

If you're not consciously focusing on what you're feeding your brain, your RAS can be hugely harmful to your goals.

In a lot of ways, I live my life by this quote from inspirational speaker, Michael Bernard Beckwith, "You attract to you the predominant thoughts that you're holding in your awareness, whether those thoughts are conscious or unconscious." In other words, you're either consciously or subconsciously locking onto things all the time. And whatever you lock onto, is what comes back to you. Armed with that knowledge, why wouldn't you actively lock onto things you want to attract? Every thought is a boomerang. I never throw anything out into the universe that I don't want to come back to me.

The good news, is that you can program your RAS to lock onto things you want to lock onto, and allow anything that isn't beneficial to your goals or general wellbeing become scotomas. Just the same as when you spent all that time researching your new car, programming your RAS is just a willful decision to surround yourself with the kinds of programming that will build you up.

Let's look at an unconsciously programmed RAS in action. Let's say you've just been tasked with reaching your quota by selling your company's worst-selling product. Your initial reaction is to lock onto all the reasons why you have the worst luck in your department. You tell yourself things like, "People don't buy this for a reason," or, "This won't help anyone improve their life," or, "There's no way I can do this." You've now locked onto a belief system that is literally shattering your goal.

You'll now seek out people who are in alignment with this belief system. Our RAS is always proving us right, even if the result is harmful to us.

The best thing to do in that moment is to empty your mind of that negative programming, and ask yourself a simple question: **How does the person who believes the opposite of what I believe think?**

They might think this is the greatest product in the world, that it helps everyone improve their life, and that they believe they have everything within them to reach their quota. This takes you into the incredible place to advocating for an opposite position of yours. It breaks your locked-on state and programs your RAS to lock onto a new goal, a new reality, a new way of seeing the world.

This can be a challenging way to reframe your perspective at first, but it's an infinitely rewarding one. Just put yourself in someone else's shoes whose mindset you want to adopt, see it from their perspective, and embody their beliefs. It's that simple.

The biggest pushback I see around this new locked-on belief, is that it somehow isn't authentic or true to you. Since you already know the authenticity argument is out the window, you're left with the truth. The presupposition here is that there's only one truth, and that one truth is that this product is objectively bad and nobody wants to buy it.

But written out like that, the logic already breaks apart, doesn't it? Of course people want to buy it. Past salespeople just haven't been able to connect it with true life improvement. But the difference is that they weren't locked onto the right mindset and blinded to the negative programming, you are. They weren't sales warriors, you are.

APPLICATION

Picture a screen door in the springtime. It lets in a cool breeze of fresh air, and keeps the bugs out of your home. Your RAS is like a screen door to your brain, but as soon as you tell yourself something negative, the bugs start to come in with the breeze.

By locking onto negatives, either consciously or subconsciously, you're allowing them to rule your results and tamper with your success. This is your RAS at work. But you can take control of your goal-seeking mechanism by moving the focus.

Right now, I want you to write out your entire day, from the time you wake up to the moment you fall asleep. This will allow you to program what you want to accomplish into your RAS.

1. What time are you waking up? What's the first thing you want to do in the morning? Maybe you want to grab a cup of coffee, or go for a morning jog? Envision your perfect start to your day.

2. Now you're on your way to work. What kind of music are you listening to? Or maybe you're playing an audiobook. Envision your perfect commute to work.

3. Imagine your entire workday if it were up to you. How would you plan out your tasks? What are you spending the most time on? How do you see yourself closing sales? Envision your ideal workday.

4. Now that your day has come to an end, how do you want to feel? What does the rest of your evening look like? Are you feeling accomplished with your day? Envision the end to a perfect day.

5. Use your vision to create the locked on state you want for your life going forward.

35

NO LOOSE ENDS

" I achieve resolution with every prospect. "

I've spent years studying top 1% salespeople, and among all the things they have in common, one in particular stands out.

Every single one of them has a resolution-focused mindset.

At its core, sales is about resolution. It's about turning uncertainty into certainty. That's why I have such a problem when I hear people say, "Selling is all about relationships". That's not the objective. There's nothing wrong with developing a relationship with your prospects, but when that becomes the goal, the sale goes sideways. If your goal is to create a relationship, then you're not actually helping them achieve life improvement. Unless resolution is the ultimate goal, you might actually be creating more ambiguity or confusion.

Sales isn't a homogenous profession. There are people from all backgrounds, creeds, faiths. But the one tie that binds the best together, is that they have a total, unwavering focus on resolving the sale. And someone who isn't focused on resolving their prospect's needs will always settle toward the bottom. It's just a truism of sales that will always, always, be the reality.

Like every company with a sales department, our CRM is constantly filled with leads. The programming I give to my salespeople is to *resolve* the sale. It's to take it to its furthest possible extent with your process, and achieve resolution. Statistically, that means that some of those sales aren't going to close. But I would rather hear "no" from a potential buyer than have the ambiguity of that sale hovering off in the distance somewhere. I truly believe that ambiguity cripples sales, and I'll do anything to make sure we have a sale resolved, in one way or the other. That way, we can move on.

So, I've found that the sales warriors who run toward that resolution, without worrying about the score, are the ones who make more sales. That's why you'll sometimes hear me chant in our office, "No loose ends."

In 1972, psychologist, Jerome Kagan, did a study and found that uncertainty resolution determines our behavior. When you don't know something, your brain is highly motivated to figure out what's going on. Kagan found that the motivation to find certainty and resolution, is also behind every other piece of motivation you have: achievement, belonging, success. Social psychologist, Arie Kruglanski, called this "cognitive closure." The definition is, "an individual's desire for a firm answer to a question, and an aversion toward ambiguity".

That's your brain. More importantly, that's your prospect's brain. It hates ambiguity, and it's doing everything it can to avoid that overwhelmed state, and find resolution. And when it doesn't find that resolution, motivation ceases, and everything else breaks down. In other words, when certainty is lost, all is lost.

So, when you do things like give your prospects to-do lists, or tell them, "I'll just be over here if you need anything", you're not driving toward resolution. You're driving toward ambiguity. You're literally going against the wiring in their brain.

When you focus on becoming their resolution, as opposed to becoming their ambiguity, you will become the sales warrior.

APPLICATION

Look at your past experiences as a series of chapters filling the book of your life. Your past chapters don't define who you will become, they just contribute to who you are at this moment. In order to live out chapters that feed into your future success, you have to take the initiative to write them.

Here's how to write your new chapter.

1. In your mind, create a new chapter in your book titled *The Sales Warrior*.

2. Label the past chapters that don't contribute to your new Sales Warrior chapter. These could be your "yielding" chapter, or your "helper" chapter, or your "relationships" chapter.

3. List all the characteristics of the new chapter you're creating. You can list out words like, "Strong", "Leader", "Compassionate", "Relentless", "Resolution-focused". Make sure they align with the mental strategies you've picked up in this book.

4. Be conscious of this new chapter you're writing, and don't revert back to "reading" your old, unhelpful life chapters. At the same time, have gratitude for your journey here, because at times, you may revert back to reading from those old chapters. But just know that you've turned the page to a new reality.

5. Identify with this new chapter, and consciously filter your daily decisions through those characteristics. If your decisions are not helping you live out your new chapter in life, you may need to reconsider those decisions.

36

VISUALIZE IT TO BECOME IT

> "I can manifest the future I want in the present."

Being mentally stuck on a problem is one of the most common experiences in the human condition. What separates a sales warrior from everyone else is that they know the techniques to get unstuck fast.

One important reason why salespeople hit a slump, or get stuck on a problem in general, is because the movie of success inside their mind's eye stopped playing.

The first problem is an easy one for either the salesperson or the coach to diagnose. The second one, is where I see solutions start to thin out. This isn't a book about process; it's about mindset. Process is vital, but trying to improve your performance by solely practicing your process is like sticking a band aid on a bullet hole. If you want to achieve your full potential, you need the mindset. You need to put in the dedication to retraining your brain to think like a sales warrior.

Visualizing success helps you accomplish three extremely important things.

1. It activates your creative subconscious, which will start generating creative ideas to achieve your goals.
2. It programs your brain to more readily perceive and recognize the resources you need to achieve your goals.
3. It builds your internal motivation to take the necessary actions to achieve your goals.

We're running movies in our head all the time. We imagine scenarios at work before they happen. We visualize tough conversations with family members before we have them. We feel the sand of the beach, and see the view of the ocean before we even get on a plane for vacation.

Just the same, sales warriors use visualization as a conscious tool to bring future goals into the present. Let's say you have a goal to double your income in a year. A sales warrior would step inside the movie of that success a year from now. They would turn up the volume and make the colors more vivid and feel it from a first-person perspective. The richer, and more realistic, those visualized internal movies are, the more likely that goal becomes a reality.

Athletes use visualization techniques all the time because it was discovered that when athletes imagine a perfect performance often enough, neural pathways become conditioned *to achieve what they've imagined.* So when you envision your own success, it will enhance your confidence and motivation, so your chances of success can be greatly multiplied.

And it makes sense, doesn't it? Highly effective sales warriors have such realistic movies playing inside their minds, that they can basically manufacture motivation out of nowhere. If you can see, feel, and hear the joy your family experiences on vacation after that major pay raise, it enhances your drive to push through that next sales call. If you know your goal is to double your salary, and you've mentally experienced it, then of course, you'll be driven to find solutions to get unstuck. It's only natural.

Golfer, Jack Nicklaus, won more major tournaments than anyone in history. He famously said, "I never hit a shot, not even in practice, without having a very sharp, in-focus picture of it in my head. First, I see the ball where I want it to finish, nice and white and sitting up high on the bright green grass. Then the scene quickly changes, and I see the ball going there; its path, trajectory, and shape, even its behavior on landing." Nicklaus credits that visualization tactic for a lot of his success.

You'll also find that visualizing strategies comes more easily as well. If you're struggling to get past a current problem, turn up the intensity of your own mental image. Visualize yourself succeeding. What did you do to give yourself that success? You'll quickly find that everything you need is within you now.

Neuro Linguistic Programming (NLP) changed my life. With the help of my incredible coach, Susan Stageman, I went on a journey to become a certified NLP Master Practitioner. It's completely shaped the way I see my relationship to others, and it's allowed me to become more effective at helping people become better versions of themselves every single day.

NLP is an approach to communication, personal development, and psychotherapy, created to help people become their best selves. A key teaching in NLP is that every experience you've ever had has a structure, just like a computer. Because of limitations to your computer, you might not be able to run some programs.

That doesn't mean you can never run those programs, it just means you need to upgrade your computer. So, if you find that your current mental computer isn't equipped with the programs to succeed in a current experience, then all you need to do is upgrade your mental computer. Visualization is one of those key upgrades.

APPLICATION

When you visualize what you really want in life, surround yourself with those images, and put in the work, you can manifest anything you want and make it true for you.

Visualization isn't a psychic power that grants you everything you want. Visualization is a technique that, when combined with hard work, will cause you to act in ways that push you towards your goal.

So, here's how to use visualization to build yourself up.

1. **Set a clear goal.** Once you have a clear goal, write it out and work backwards from the moment you achieved your goal to create a path. Write each preceding event that needs to happen before you can reach this goal.

2. **Gather inspiration.** Find images that will remind you of your purpose every single day. These images can be of people you want to be like, people you love, people who have inspired you, places you want to go, places that remind you of your goal. The images you use can be anything that will give your goal a tangible picture.

3. **Put your images somewhere you will see them and be reminded every single day.** Maybe you want to keep your visual in your wallet and carry it with you everywhere. Maybe you want to keep your visual on your desk at work, or on your bathroom mirror where you will see it every morning. No matter where you decide to store your tangible goal, make sure you see it every single day.

    Bonus: Put the visualizations in places you don't normally go. It's easy to think about your goal when you're at work, or when you're starting your day, but you don't always think about your goals when you open a kitchen cabinet or drive to the grocery store. The more continuous your visualization, the better the technique will work.

4. **Be mindful.** The key to successfully achieving a goal with the visualization technique, is to be mindful about it. Don't just look at

the image and say "OK, there's my goal." Look at your images and repeat your goal to yourself every day.

5. **Take massive action.** You have the knowledge, you have skills, and you have the opportunity, but none of it matters unless you take massive action and execute.

37

THE DOWNSTREAM MIND

> "I control every situation because I'm the most flexible element in that situation."

"Just go with the flow."

"It's all downstream from here."

I've heard these phrases hundreds of times in my life, and I know I've said them to others as well. But do we know what these sayings actually mean? Or where they have their origin?

Esther Hicks is an inspirational speaker and author, and she co-wrote nine books with her husband, Jerry Hicks. She's also presented numerous Abraham Hicks workshops on the Law of Attraction, and I love their explanation of upstream and downstream thoughts.

Basically, we live our lives going either with or against the flow of a stream. The stream is always taking us towards the things we want, to the fulfillment of all of our desires. But a lot of times, we fight the stream because we get too wrapped up in the negative thoughts and stories that we tell ourselves. We think, "I'm actually not sure I like this stream, I'd rather go in this direction," and now life becomes an upstream slog. You're fighting reality. But imagine the relief you'd feel if you suddenly stopped paddling, and let the current take you.

Having a downstream mind is all about releasing the resistance to circumstances that we've created in our heads. Think about the flow of traffic. Imagine you're sitting in gridlock, and you look beside you, and you see someone smashing their fists on their dashboard, slamming on their horn, and smashing on the accelerator and brake every time traffic inches forward. How much negative mental energy is that person expending by turning traffic into an upstream fight? Instead, you know better. You flip on an empowering podcast, or audiobook, or pump-up music, and you go with the flow. I know who's arriving to work in a more productive mood.

Whenever I see someone's selling process go down the tubes, I can usually trace it back to a single idea: they turned a downstream sale into an upstream struggle.

It's the same concept in selling. The basic premise is that you never want to stop your own sale. So, you'll almost never hear me say the word "no" in the course of a sale. Instead, you'll hear me say **"yes, and"**.

One of the core presuppositions of Neuro Linguistic Programming (NLP), the science of persuasive communication, is that the most flexible element in any system controls that system. This applies directly to sales. If you're openly struggling with your prospects, guess what happens? They won't be your prospects for very long.

But, if you're downstream with them, meaning you don't create any friction regardless of what they say, then you're constantly keeping the sale moving forward. Think of it like fishing. If you don't give the line slack while the fish is struggling, what happens? The line breaks.

So, let's say a prospect throws out a price objection. The answer isn't to lock into a defensive, argumentative mode to handle that objection. Don't fight the current of that stream. Embrace its direction, and accept the way the conversation has gone. The answer is to say something like, "**Yes, and** I definitely want to get to that question. So, let me show you why our value is the industry leader and we can talk more about that." See how different a conversation that is?

You may be asking yourself, "Am I a downstream person?" Here are four questions to find out.

1. Do you look forward to moments that allow you to embrace change? Or do you flee from it?
2. When you're asked to make changes, what's your first thought? Are you open? Angry? Cautious?
3. Can you live in the tension of the unknown? Or do you feel the need to control outcomes?
4. Would others say you need control? Why do you believe they think that?

There's a well-known Chinese proverb that says, "The wise adapt themselves to circumstances, as water molds itself to a pitcher." I can always tell a sales warrior because they can stay adaptable and downstream while sticking to their process.

In his book, *Everyday Survival*, author, Laurence Gonzales, talks about the unnecessary mistakes we make when we work from a mental script that doesn't match the requirements of real-world situations. In other words, when we try to fight upstream.

He explains that one of the reasons we do this, is because of how we process new information. It creates what he calls "behavior scripts", or mental models, that automate every action you take.

We build these scripts based on experiences we have, and eventually, the actions we take become second nature. For example, you learned how to button up your shirt when you were a kid, and now you can do it without having to concentrate. Even if a radically new and easier way of buttoning up shirts was created, your brain will still pull you toward the old way because it's used to that pattern. Even if it's less beneficial.

The problem this creates, is that you lock onto a script that might not be right for the situation. If your script says a conversation with a prospect should go a certain way, and it doesn't, then the answer isn't to subconsciously lean back on that script, it's to go with the flow. Just like water flowing around a boulder, your goal is to handle the objection and come out still using your process on the other side.

This requires forethought. It requires using your visualization techniques to see all the possible angles of the sale. It requires supportive self-talk. It requires a selling process that allows you to be downstream. That way, when the prospect takes a sudden sharp left turn off the trail, you can join them step for step to get them back on the right path.

APPLICATION

Whatever success you've had in the past, the best way to be downstream about it is to "steal the feeling", and use it to fuel your future success. These two repeatable steps will give you that ability in any situation.

1. Write out how you felt during times when you've achieved goals in the past. What did you do? How did you accomplish those goals? What did it feel like when you crossed the finish line?

2. Insert the goal you want into that picture, retaining the feeling you had in the past. Anchor the feeling of your past success with the mental picture of your future success. You anchor things by getting a firm picture in your mind of what you see, feel, and hear in that moment. Create a full experience around it, and you'll see that in the future.

3. Live in that moment. See, feel, and hear what it's like to succeed in that moment.

4. Use this visualization technique to give you the courage to take the next steps in obtaining the future you desire.

38

LET YOUR LIGHT SHINE

> **I am an unstoppable force who inspires others to be unstoppable.**

In a lot of ways, I've tried to live my life by this quote from author, Marianne Williamson, in her groundbreaking book, *A Return to Love*.

"Our deepest fear is not that we are inadequate. Our deepest fear is that we are powerful beyond measure. It is our light, not our darkness that most frightens us. We ask ourselves, 'Who am I to be brilliant, gorgeous, talented, fabulous?' Actually, who are you not to be?...Your playing small does not serve the world. There is nothing enlightened about shrinking so that other people won't feel

insecure around you. We are all meant to shine, as children do…It's not just in some of us; it's in everyone. And as we let our own light shine, we unconsciously give other people permission to do the same. As we are liberated from our own fear, our presence automatically liberates others."

The part I always pick out is the parting shot: **"And as we let our own light shine, we unconsciously give other people permission to do the same. As we are liberated from our own fear, our presence automatically liberates others."** Culturally, we struggle with this concept. Many of us were raised to consciously avoid sharing our successes. Anything else, we're often taught, would make others feel somehow inadequate or less-than.

Like Williamson, I believe it's actually the opposite, so long as it's done from a place of genuineness and not ego. The best reputation I can have as a sales warrior is to be known as a person of positive influence and positive energy. By consciously letting my light shine as a sales warrior, I can show others that if I'm capable of achieving something, so are you.

Your prospects are constantly giving you permission to let your light shine. When they ask for a discount because your competitor is offering one, a sales warrior believes that they're not really asking for you to give them the discount. All they're saying is, "Give me value." This is your invitation. You can respond, "I can do you even better than that. I'll give you permission to spend what we're charging. Here's why people spend that money with us to gain genuine life improvement."

At FPG, we always encourage ourselves and each other to "be the light." We believe in sharing our successes from a place of authenticity and compassion. As a leader, a parent, and a friend, I want to be known as a person of positive influence and positive energy and let my light shine into the people I care about. I want to show everyone around me that if I'm capable of success, so are they.

My dad is a great example of this. In my eyes as a kid, he was an unmatched salesperson. As a small business owner of a jewelry store, he always had the customer's best interests at heart. If someone was stretching their budget too thin to buy an engagement ring that was too expensive, he'd tell them, "I don't want you to start off your marriage on bad economic footing. So here's what we'll do. Instead of the $25,000 ring, I'm going to sell you the $10,000 ring. As you earn more over your life, you can bring your ring in, and you can trade up to a more expensive ring. And I won't mark down the value of your current ring, either."

Wow. The light my dad shined not only to his customers, but to me, was obvious for all to see. I still tell that story to friends and acquaintances because to me, that's salesmanship with the customer's best interests at heart. And what's more? It helped his sales too.

Here's how you become the light, whether it's for your prospects, your loved ones, or yourself.

1. Let go of your fear of success.

People are scared to succeed. We want to perform at the level that we expect for ourselves because it makes us feel safe. And whenever we move up a level, we start to panic. We fear that people will find out we aren't what they believe we are, or that the expectations of us will rise. To be the light, you need to release this fear and increase your expectations of yourself. Never settle and keep raising the bar. This is what will inspire the people around you.

2. Be your own light.

We can't pour from an empty cup. You need to be a light for yourself before you can be a light to anyone else. I would never be able to be the light to the people around me if I didn't have any myself. Whenever I struggle to find my inner light, I take time to meditate or talk to someone I care for about whatever it is that I'm struggling with. As we transform into a pillar of light, we become a source of inspiration to everyone we meet.

3. Start listening.

You can shine your light as a sales warrior by putting aside your viewpoint and validating your customer's perspective. Sometimes, you're the light by being a leader. Other times, you shine for someone by just listening and being present. Always aim to make people feel big, that's how you get the sale.

The bottom line is that you're an unstoppable force as a sales warrior. If you doubt this, the question isn't to ask, "How am I an unstoppable force?" The question to ask is, "How am I *not* an unstoppable force?"

When you become the unstoppable force, you become the sales warrior.

APPLICATION

Studies show that by simply changing your language, you can change the chemistry of your brain. If you use negative words and phrases, your brain will think more cynically, and you'll limit your growth. Use more positive words, and you're more likely to achieve your goals.

This is one of the best ways to make sure you're constantly letting your light shine by removing any fear of success you might have within you now.

1. Pick 5 words from this list of high-achiever words that you don't currently use frequently. Commit to adding these to your daily vocabulary for the next seven days and working them into sentences you use. Feel free to come up with more on your own as well. High-achiever word examples:

   - Possibility
   - Opportunity
   - Grateful
   - Curious
   - Purpose
   - Powerful
   - Perseverance
   - Strength
   - Finesse
   - Leader
   - Inspire
   - Guide
   - Excellence
   - Breakthrough
   - Milestone
   - Victory

2. Every day, reflect back on your results and your frame of mind after adding these words to your vocabulary. As you become more comfortable using them, be conscious about continuing to add in more.

39

WARRIOR MEDITATION

> "I can use my mind to change my circumstances."

Meditation has surged in popularity in the last few years. Physical therapists, counselors, and teachers even started using meditation techniques to help their patients and students. But what exactly is meditation? It's not just sitting on the floor with your eyes closed, and it's definitely not an excuse to take a nap in the middle of your day.

Meditation is an act of intentionally employing your attention in different ways to create internal balance. Meditation balances your brain and body in the same way a scuba diver equalizes the pressure in their masks as they dive deeper. It's nothing more than intentionally going inside your own mind, and giving yourself the gift of awareness for what's inside of you.

Dr. Joe Dispenza is an award-winning researcher who's spent his life teaching others how to rewire their brains and completely change their reality. In his book, *Breaking the Habit of Being Yourself*, he said this about meditation: "Meditating is a means for you to move beyond your analytical mind so that you can access your subconscious mind. That's crucial, since the subconscious is where all your bad habits and behaviors that you want to change reside."

Sometimes our deepest fear in meditation isn't the practice itself, but what we'll find when we do go inside our subconscious mind. Our own thoughts can be our worst enemy. I used to blast music through my headphones all the time, not because I loved the music, but because I wanted to escape my own thoughts. Meditation changed everything for me. I no longer had to drown out the thoughts inside my head because meditation cleared the clutter out of my brain. Now I was engaging with my thoughts, or disarming them, but never running from them.

Your conscious mind is stuffed with everything inside your awareness. It's filled to the brim with every sensation, perception, memory, feeling, and fantasy you've ever accumulated over time. We all know psychologist, Sigmund Freud, had some pretty wild theories, but his explanation of the conscious mind, is the best way to understand what it truly is. He explained that your personality is like an iceberg, and the tip of the iceberg above the water represents your conscious mind. Beneath the water's surface is where the bulk of the iceberg hides, and that represents your subconscious mind.

Simply put, the things that are hidden from your awareness exert the greatest influence over your personality and behaviors.

Meditation is the key to unlocking your subconscious mind so you can fully embody who you are. That's why it's one of the first things I do in my morning ritual every day when I wake up. I have to connect with myself to know that I can make the most of each day. Otherwise I'm being pulled in many different directions by forces outside my control.

The scientific benefits of meditation are undeniable. It helps your brain to sharpen your attention span, increases your resiliency to stress, increases compassion, and even has a positive impact on your physical health. The more consistently I meditate, the more centered and healthy I become.

All of these things help with your sales career. Meditating has been scientifically proven by the US National Library of Medicine to improve your ability to make decisions. It rewires your brain to improve the functioning of your brain's decision-making centers by cutting out the bombarding noise of daily life. It also improves your memory, allowing you to store and utilize more information – like what you're learning in this book.

As you already know, people naturally run off their programming. Your programming may tell you that if a prospect is frowning and crossing their arms, they're not interested in buying. When you just give in to this kind of programming, your brain is doing everything it can to make it come true. It becomes a self-fulfilling prophecy that you tell yourself over, and over again.

Whatever programming, negative beliefs, or fears that you have around yourself, or your role as a salesperson, meditation allows you to unlock the truth in your subconscious. This incredible tool will help you detach from your conscious mind, and dive into the truth of any situation, feeling, or belief that you experience.

By making this a regular practice, you'll notice not just your emotional wellbeing increase, but you'll see physical benefits too, in the form of decreased stress, and anxiety, and increased confidence.

Life will throw giant waves at your metaphorical boat. You already know that. The salespeople who don't make it are the ones who aren't self-aware enough to notice the change in the weather.

APPLICATION

The purpose of meditation is to lower your brain waves, so that you can re-direct your attention from external noise, to the internal truth. These steps will help you access your subconscious mind, which could only happen through meditation practices.

1. Get in a quiet place free of distraction, and begin counting down from 10 to 1. Your goal is to control your mind to where the only thing you're focused on, is the number in your head.

2. Any time you think of anything at all, aside from the number you're currently counting, start over at 10.

3. Once you finish this process successfully, then launch into a clear-minded meditative state where you can allow your mind to create awareness and solutions for you.

4. As you get more comfortable counting down from 10, increase the number to 15, then 20, and so on. Eventually, you'll become more and more comfortable shutting out distractions for longer periods of time.

40

FIND YOUR FLOW

"I am the master of the current moment."

Think about a Red Bull athlete with wings strapped to their back, soaring through tight windows of rock in the mountains. How are they able to succeed without taking a millimeter turn and crashing head-first into the mountain?

It's because they're in a heightened state of flow. And you can access the same deeply focused state as the most thrill-seeking Red Bull athlete on the planet right now. All it takes is mindfulness.

In Steven Kotler's book, *The Rise of Superman*, he defines flow like this: "Flow is an optimal state of consciousness, a peak state where we feel our best and perform our best." Put even more simply, flow is any moment where you're so focused on the task at hand that you're able to shut out distractions and fall into a place of pure productivity. For an athlete we might call this "in the zone," when they seem so locked in that they can't miss. Like Kobe Bryant scoring 81 points in a game, or Tom Brady engineering a 25-point comeback in the Super Bowl.

In Kotler's book, he found that executives are 500% more productive in a state of flow, and U.S. military snipers in flow learned concepts 200-500% faster than other troops. He also found that there are four primary triggers to getting into flow: psychological, environmental, social, and creative. By accessing those four flow channels, top producers were able to block out distractions, drop into a productive state, and outperform their peers.

> **Psychological:** Internally driven triggers that focus you on the present task at hand.
>
> **Environmental:** Externally driven triggers that pull from your surroundings to get you into flow.
>
> **Social:** Triggers focused on finding flow as part of a larger group.
>
> **Creative:** Triggers focused on risk-taking and hard-charging activities.

Flow is such an effective method for sales warriors because it hijacks the brain's amygdala. The amygdala is the brain's primal fight, flee, or freeze mechanism. This is especially harmful to sales warriors because all three will damage the sales process: fighting with the prospect, fleeing from the sale, or freezing when objections come up are all fatal outcomes.

Flow gives you something I call "The Fourth F:" Freedom. It allows you to respond to the situation, not just react in a purely primal way. Think of it like having relaxed focus, where everything around you slows down, and you can handle every issue as it comes. That's what being in flow feels like.

For instance, I know my flow state is something Kotler calls "hard charger". This means I get into my optimal flow state, by thriving on intense situations. That's why I gravitate toward things like high-intensity morning workouts, Spartan Races, and ziplines. When I feel like I'm challenging myself in that way, I know I can activate my flow, so I make sure to incorporate those into my routine.

And so I actively look to find those things during my day. In our corporate headquarters, I have Red Bull TV playing at all times. I surround myself with imagery like samurai swords, and Roman-era armor. I've recognized within myself that when I can activate the hard charger within me, I can activate my flow any time I want.

Just the same, you can engineer your own life around your flow state. Do you get into flow in a quiet room with limited distractions? Do you thrive when you're surrounded by a buzzing hive of activity? The more quickly you can identify how you get yourself into flow, the better you can optimize your day and your results.

APPLICATION

As you've already learned, there are four primary triggers to finding your optimal flow state: psychological, environmental, social, and creative.

I use a creative flow trigger every morning:

Determine what that is for you. What do you do that makes you feel as though you're performing at your highest level? Create a plan to consistently engage in that for the next 90 days.

Once you're in a state of flow, you'll know it. You'll be fully immersed in a feeling of energized focus, full involvement, and enjoyment in the process of the activity. Some people get deep into their flow state when they are working with other people collaboratively, while others get into flow by surrounding themselves in complete silence and solitude.

As you consciously discover your optimal flow state, follow these three vital criteria.

1. **Determine your flow trigger.**

    Psychological: Internally driven flow triggers that focus you on the present task at hand.

    Environmental: Externally-driven triggers that pull from your surroundings to get you into flow.

    Social: Flow triggers focused on finding flow as part of a larger group.

    Creative: Flow triggers focused on risk-taking and hard-charging activity.

2. **Find the importance.** What about that flow state is important to you? How will it help you increase your results? What will it do for you? What are things you can do to live into that flow state and hit your flow trigger more often?

3. **Add to your routine.** Before you start any big task, or get your day going, be intentional about adding resources around your flow trigger. Be intentional and act.

I have a short, high-intensity workout because my brain craves the energy and focus that workout time creates.

41

BECOME THE ULTIMATE ENERGY SOURCE

"I maximize both my feminine and masculine energy."

Right now, no matter your gender, you have two energy poles within you: your purest masculine energy is on one pole, and your purest feminine energy is on the other.

No matter who you are, you're naturally pulled toward one energy pole over the other. Sometimes it's gender-based, like when men project more masculine energy, and women project more feminine energy. But sometimes it's not. Either way, modern research shows that every human being has both masculine and feminine energy within them. So the idea that having primarily feminine energy as a man or masculine energy as a woman is a weakness is simply not true. It's a strength to have both, not a weakness. And it's neither a strength nor a weakness to be dominant in one over the other, no matter what your gender is.

In alignment with sales, feminine energy skews toward creativity, collaboration, and flexibility. Masculine energy, meanwhile, skews more toward resolution, achievement and authority. Society programs us to believe that every male is dominant in male-specific energies, and every female is dominant in female-specific energies. That causes salespeople to typecast their prospects or, even worse, not pay attention to energy at all and let programming take over. In other words, if you only use masculine or feminine energy with prospects who need both, you're losing sales because of it.

The latest research conducted by Daphna Joel, a professor of neuroscience at Tel Aviv University, found that you are a biological mixture of masculine and feminine features.

After analyzing the brains of more than 1,400 men and women, Joel didn't find a single consistent difference between the sexes. Instead she found that we are all a unique blend of masculine and feminine energy. Her study discovered that between 0-8% of people had brains that would be considered "all" male or "all" female. The vast majority of people were somewhere in the middle, meaning that gender energy isn't a one-or-the-other thing. We're all a mixture of both.

Just the same, research from professor, Simon Baron-Cohen, a psychologist at Cambridge University, found that about 59% of the human race is energy neutral. That means that roughly 4.1 billion people on earth relate to the world with about equal masculine and feminine energy.

Right now, I want you to think of your sales energy like a horizontal line. On one pole, you have extreme masculine speed. This is the super aggressive salesperson who's just trying to churn out sale after sale without gaining rapport with the customer. This kind of behavior is where a lot of the unethical stereotypes of overly aggressive salespeople come from. It's not customer mission focused. It's purely transactional.

And on the complete opposite side of the pole, you have extreme feminine flexibility. This is the more creative, collaborative energy that wants to back off the sale and give the buyer an infinite number of options. This might sound like, "You know, I'm just here to help you. So, let me show you absolutely everything we sell, and you can figure out what's right for you."

So, pure speed energy is too aggressive, it puts prospects in a defensive posture. And the pure flexibility energy is too passive, it puts prospects in this overwhelmed state where they lock up and can't make a decision. So what do you do? You balance your energy by giving a blend of speed and flexibility to every prospect.

So right now I want you to think about it – with just about every sale you've ever lost, you could place yourself on an extreme end of one of these poles. Either you were too aggressive, and you went straight for the close before you got position of strength and rapport. Or, you were too flexible, and the prospect got so overwhelmed by their options that they gave up.

When you're in a selling situation, you need to match the energy of your prospect, so that you can be aligned before you lead them through the sale. I'm sure you've experienced a misalignment of energies before, you probably just didn't realize it. When you're fighting with your coworker, and one of you is trying to calmly listen while the other wants to shout, you'll never meet resolution. You need to match the energy of the other person so you can take control of the situation.

Since we all have both masculine and feminine energies inside of us, then the pathway to becoming a sales warrior is obvious: by balancing both within yourself, you'll be able to connect with any customer's energy as well.

The selling process is a fundamental mixture of compassion and strength, connection and achievement, caring and authority. This is the exact kind of blended energy that moves sales forward.

APPLICATION

You want to be able to utilize both your masculine and feminine energy depending on the prospect in front of you.

1. Take 5 minutes out of every day and quietly allow any and all emotions to come to the surface. Focus on your emotional state, and don't hold anything back. Focus on removing any barriers keeping you from experiencing your emotion.

2. Pick one masculine or feminine emotion you feel, and focus on that emotion alone for the next 5 minutes. Concentrate on how that emotion makes you feel, both physically and psychologically.

3. Consciously "stop" the emotion for the next 24 hours before "turning it back on." This just means focusing on consciously keeping that emotion at bay at will.

The purpose of this exercise is to be able to turn on and off an emotion when you need to. So, if you only access your masculine energy, you want to be able to bring feminine energy to the forefront when you need it. If you want more of one or the other in a selling situation, you'll be able to "turn on" that emotion when you need it as it benefits you.

All energies are good. The purpose is to keep them from controlling you.

42

BREAK THE HABIT LOOP

"I control my own response to any situation."

You've reached the final mental strategy of this book. And it's the final strategy for a very good reason.

Now that you've added all these new mental tools to your arsenal, it's time to learn how to sharpen each one by creating beneficial habits around them. Each of these mental toughness strategies will increase your income and improve your life, but only if you commit to incorporating them into your daily routines. And the way you incorporate each one, is by creating a habit loop around them.

When I decided to get fit enough to run a Spartan Race, I didn't just arrive at it overnight. Some mornings I didn't want that high intensity workout before I rolled into the office. I wanted the reward of hitting the snooze button and getting an extra 30 minutes of rest.

After learning from Charles Duhigg and his book, *The Power of Habit*, I committed to creating a habit loop around it. I stopped hitting snooze one day, and the next, and the next. It became a pattern. Now I can't go without any workout, and I'm in a healthier state than I've ever been. That's the power of the habit loop.

Everyone has negative triggers. The difference between sales warriors, and everyone else, is that sales warriors are bigger than their triggers.

The habit loop is how we create our habitual behaviors. First, you experience a trigger, then you give a response, and you get an emotional reward at the end. So, let's look at it through a selling lens. First the trigger hits: the prospect says they're not sure they want to buy, so they're going to think about their options for a while. Your response comes out, "No problem, I understand, let me know if you ever make a decision." The reward is that you feel good because you feel like you did what you needed to do to help the prospect.

So, what's wrong with that picture? It's not the trigger. You can't control their reaction, it was your response to the trigger.

One thing you already realize, is that you can't change the front end of the loop. You can't control the trigger. And the way you respond to the trigger governs the reward you get at the end. If you do something wrong, for instance, like run into another car, there's no reward involved, so the habit loop never forms.

So, let's go back to our previous selling example. The prospect hits your trigger by saying they've decided to leave and think it over. You want that reward – you know you want to leave that conversation feeling like you've moved them toward resolution.

Your response controls your mentality. You *will* have triggers; the question is whether you see it, and overcome those triggers, or not. So, if you tell the prospect, "Don't worry about it, hope to see you again when you make a decision," then you have a warped sense of what your reward really is. Helping the prospect isn't letting them go, leaving them to their own self-doubt, ambiguity, and confusion. Helping the prospect is explaining how what you sell is the one thing that will pull them out of that ambiguous place. You need to identify what you missed in the process that lead them to remain in this state. Let this statement further peak your curiosity. That's a much better way to lead yourself to a reward than simply letting them leave.

Having awareness around your triggers is key. Maybe you notice within yourself that you wait for your prospect to smile, or give you some positive feedback, before you launch into your selling message. That's an example of how a misplaced trigger can limit your sales. Or, an objection could trigger a mental off-switch, causing you to quit the sale before you've had a chance to handle the objection. Within yourself, you need to identify these triggers, understand them, and eliminate them.

Right now, you may be thinking, "But Jason, how do I know whether a response is negative or not? How do I figure out which responses to change?" I would look at this very simply; is your response helping you move sales forward or not? The primary question of every sales warrior is, how can I move a sale forward today? That's it – that's your litmus.

So you want to pick out any responses that stop you from doing what you know to do 100% of the time. If your response leads to inaction, that's a leash. If it creates anxiety or fear in your selling message, that's a leash. If it's preventing you from exceeding your sales quota so you can take your family on that vacation you've been talking about, that's a leash. Just focus on controlling what you can control, and let the score take care of itself.

By knowing how you respond to certain objections or comments, you'll know your old, familiar habit loops creeping up when it happens. If you respond a certain way to every trigger, then you can have conscious awareness around that, and change your response. You can break your habit loop.

When you control your response, you control the sale. It's as simple as that.

APPLICATION

When left alone, habit loops can form destructive trigger responses with good intentions. The trigger is a time of uncertainty or anxiety, and in order to get to the positive reward, the response must be in alignment with your identity as a sales warrior. Having awareness around this habit loop process will change the game for how you respond to difficult triggers.

1. Train yourself to notice your trigger in the moment. It could be a phrase you hear, or a selling situation you find yourself in. What feeling does this trigger bring out in you? How is it affecting the way you look at yourself, your prospect, your situation?

2. Change your response. Instead of reaching for your programmed response (procrastination, complaining, a limiting belief) reach for this book. Find a mental strategy that helps you the most for that particular situation, commit yourself to mastering that strategy, and apply it to your trigger.

3. Keep your reward the same. If your reward is resolution and peace, make that the same reward after submitting yourself to a new strategy in this book. The result is that the reward stays the same, but your response improves.

A WARRIOR SEND-OFF

You are now a broker of sales warrior strategies.

I've given you these strategies because I believe the greatest gift you can give anyone, is the gift of freedom. These are your mental tools to have the freedom of a sales warrior, and when you incorporate these into your daily mental practice, they will improve both your life, and the lives of your customers. It's as simple as that.

But on a deeper level, the purpose of these strategies is to give you freedom by giving you choice. By simultaneously patching the leaks, and expanding your mental bucket size, you're expanding the amount of new information, knowledge, and understanding you can take in. And when your bucket size improves, your results expand as well. This is just as true in every other area of your life as it is in sales.

So, commit to using this as your mental sales guide. Keep these strategies close to you at all times. Pull from individual chapters when you need them. Be conscious about your growth. Celebrate yourself. Give yourself compassion. Understand that you now have the green light to become a better version of you every day.

If you're interested in learning more about sales and leadership programs built around these mental toughness techniques, visit us at **www.FPG.com**. Learning is a journey, and we pride ourselves on guiding our clients through that journey of strengthening their mind, so they can achieve anything in life. Not just in their sales, but in every aspect.

Now that you see things differently, commit to sharing a strategy, or multiple, with someone who needs to be as unleashed and liberated as you now are. I believe at the end of everyone's lives, we'll be judged on the answers to two questions: who did I **become**, and what did I **contribute**? Your life is all about making a difference in others' lives. With these strategies, you're now empowered to be the difference-maker.

You have everything within you now to become the sales warrior. All it takes is a decision. Your unleashed life starts now. Are you ready to begin?

CPSIA information can be obtained
at www.ICGtesting.com
Printed in the USA
BVHW061938241019
562030BV00003B/7/P